Interpreting Poetry and Evaluating Criticism

Bijay Kumar Das

ATLANTIC

PUBLISHERS & DISTRIBUTORS (P) LTD

Published by

ATLANTIC

PUBLISHERS & DISTRIBUTORS (P) LTD

7/22, Ansari Road, Darya Ganj, New Delhi-110002
Phones : +91-11-40775252, 40775214, 23273880, 23275880
Fax : +91-11-23285873
Web : www.atlanticbooks.com
E-mail : orders@atlanticbooks.com

Branch Office: Chennai
Phones : +91-44-48531784, 28291383
E-mail : chennai@atlanticbooks.com

Printed & bound in India by Atlantic Print Services

For

Nissim Ezekiel, who paved the way
in admiration and gratitude

Preface

To interpret poetry is to dive deep into the core of it so as to evaluate it. Criticism is inevitable in order to understand a poem. Apart from "Introduction", the book contains 10 chapters equally divided into two parts. Part I seeks to interpret British, Irish and Indian English poets for the benefit of the readers. The poets who figure in the section are W.B. Yeats, T.S. Eliot, Seamus Heaney, Ted Hughes, Nissim Ezekiel, A.K. Ramanujan, Kamala Das, Keki N. Daruwalla, Jayanta Mahapatra, Shiv K. Kumar, Dom Moraes and Jeet Thayil. Part II is devoted to Indian English criticism and Western criticism. The relation between the author and the text, critical canon, glocalization and postcolonial theory have been evaluated for the benefit of students, scholars and teachers, of Indian universities.

In the end, a select bibliography has been given, both by way of acknowledgement, and by the way of bringing to the notice of the readers the materials available in the field. Index has also been provided for quick access to different topics.

I would like to thank Dr. K.R. Gupta and the staff of Atlantic Publishers & Distributors (P) Ltd. for publishing the book in record time.

Burdwan University, Burdwan **Bijay Kumar Das**

Acknowledgements

Acknowledgements are due to the following journals in which some of the chapters of this book first appeared: *The Critical Endevour; The Literary Criterion; Points of View; Journal of the Department of English*, Burdwan University, Burdwan; and *Journal of Indian Writing in English*.

Bijay Kumar Das

Contents

PART–I

1

Introduction

The origin of poetry is as old as the origin of mankind. People began telling stories and singing songs from time immemorial. The oral poetry continued to be sung from generation to generation across the world. Then came the poetry in the written form in various scripts of different world languages. Interpretation of poetry came much later with the division of it into several forms—ballads, epics, elegies and songs of love and death. Originally thought to be a source of joy and matter of delight, poetry began to be read for meaning. There in comes the question of interpretation.

In earlier ages, say from the fourteenth century to the nineteenth century, poetry was analysed in terms of various forms such as epic, sonnet, ode, elegy, satire and also on the basis of the concepts of romanticism, classicism and finally modernism. Love, death, time, nature, god, beauty, art, heaven and hell continued to be the subject of poetry. And then came the twentieth century. T.S. Eliot, I.A. Richards and F.R. Leavis gave a new direction to the interpretation of poetry. C.B. Cox and A.E. Dyson have traced the course of interpretation of poetry in the following words:

> In *The Muse Unchained* (1958), E.M.W. Tillyard has described how in the post-1918 period the teachers at Cambridge wanted to supplant this imprecise laudatory criticism by something more rigorous. Particularly influential was I.A. Richards, whose famous book, *Practical Criticism* was published in 1929 (9).

Besides, Richards three other critics T.S. Eliot, F.R. Leavis and William Empson have altered the traditional method of analysis of poetry through their writings. Eliot's idea of 'unification of sensibility', 'dissociation of sensibility', 'objective correlative', and his *Selected Essays* (1932 rpt. 1951). F.R. Leavis's journal, *Scrutiny* (1932), William Empson's *Seven Types of Ambiguity* (1930) have revolutionalized interpretation of poetry in the twentieth century.

Eliot's essay "The Metaphysical Poets" (1921) included in *Selected Essays* (1932) contains two brilliant ideas, 'unification of sensibility' and 'dissociation of sensibility'. A great poem occurs in when the sensibility is unified as it is in John Donne. Emotion and intellect are harmoniously blended together when heart and head become one. "A thought to Donne was an experience, it modified his sensibility," says Eliot. But in the seventeenth century with Milton and Dryden 'a dissociation of sensibility set in'. Here emotion is separated from intellect, the schism between head and heart is loudly pronounced. Leavis is with Eliot as far as unified sensibility is concerned.

> For Leavis and his followers, analysis was not merely a technique for precise description of literature, but a process whereby the reader could 'cultivate awareness', and grow towards the unified sensibility. Analysis was necessary because a poem resulted from a complex of associated feelings and thoughts. A great poem was not a simple, forceful statement of some well-known experience, 'What oft was thought, but ne'er so well express'd', but a profoundly original creation only fully comprehended after close textual analysis (Cox and Dyson 12).

Ezra Pound and T.S. Eliot laid emphasis on images. For them image becomes the idea. Experiences are better expressed in images not in words. French symbolists led by Mallarme influenced both Pound and Eliot to take the image seriously and find out its impact on the poem. In the words of C.B. Cox and A.E. Dyson "the image in a poem gave the reader a moment of illumination beyond normal apprehension and so introduced him to a kind of sensibility not to be found in everyday living" (13). Here we are reminded of Eliot's theory of "Objective Correlative" in which Eliot expressed his opinion that in order to express an experience we need not merely the language but an image through which it is to be realized. In other words, Eliot, and Leavis shifted the emphasis from meaning to realization achieved in the poem. Here I am reminded of T.S. Eliot's statement in his memorial lecture on W.B. Yeats when he said that the great poet is man who "Out of intense and personal experience is able to express a general truth: retaining all the particularity of his experience to make of it a general symbol" (Cullingford 76).

Then came the New Critics, who sought the metaphorical meaning of the poem by laying emphasis on tropes and figurative language. Irony, paradox and ambiguity became the norm of interpreting poetry. The hidden (oblique) meaning of the poem sought to be unearthed by solving ambiguity (thanks to Empson) in the poem. Here, I am reminded of Allen Tate's statement, "Never have poetry and criticism in English been so close together" (214). If we go by Stylistics each word has several significations but the value of it is to be found in the context of the poem. 'Signification' and 'realisation' became two key words for the interpretation of poetry in the modern age (i.e., in the twentieth century). V.K. Chari makes a valid observation in this context:

> Language functions stylistically in a context, and acquires poetic meaning and force and becomes a dramatic 'gesture'. Every poem, long (such as *Paradise Lost*) or short (such as Herrick's 'Poetry of Dress') establishes its own dramatic context or situation...poetic meaning is contextual.... The range of meaning of a word, its suggestive power as well as 'delimitation', is determined by its context, which includes drift, tone, speaker, gesture, emphasis, etc. (*IJES* 19-20)

Apart from the contextual meaning, there is also scope for the poet to put the meaning in the central argument of a poem (particularly a metaphysical poem). A few quotations from John Donne's love poetry will suffice:

> Let Sea-discoverers to new worlds have gone,
> Let Maps to others, worlds on worlds have showne,

Let us possesse our world, each hath one, and is one.

("The Good-Morrow")

Love, all alike, no season knows, nor clyme
Nor houres, dayes, months, which are the rags of time.

("The Sunne Rising")

We'are Tapers too, and at our owne cost die, ...
Wee dye and rise the same, and prove
Mysterious by this love.

("The Canonization")

Philosophical meanings achieve universality in poetry as we find in Shakespeare, Pope and Eliot. Here are a few examples:

Life's but a walking shadow.
... It's a tale
Told by an idiot, full of sound and fury, signifying nothing.

(*Macbeth*)

We are such staff
As dreams are made on, and our little life
Is rounded with a sleep.

(*The Tempest*)

Know then thyself, presume not God to scan
The proper study of mankind is Man.

("Know Then Thyself"
from *An Essay on Man*)

A little learning is a dangerous thing:
Drink deep, or taste not the Pierian Spring.

(*An Essay on Criticism*)

In a minute there is time
For decisions and revisions which a minute will reverse.

("The Love Son of J. Alfred Prufrock")

The world turns and the world changes,
But one thing does not change...
The perpetual struggle of Good and Evil.

("Choruses from 'The Rock'")

> But to apprehend
> The point of intersection of the timeless
> With time, is an occupation for the saint—
>
> ("The Dry Salvages")

> The only wisdom we can hope to acquire
> Is the wisdom of humility: humility is endless.
>
> ("East Coker")

The form of poetry is no less important than the content. Figured language, assonance, rhyme, rhythm make poetry what it is today and in a way help us to distinguish it from other modes of writing—drama, fiction and non-fiction prose. 'Pun' is a useful device in poetry. Ambiguity, irony and paradox, make poetry, what it is today. Following the New historicists, the readers started interpreting poetry by going to the roots of it. Individual words lost their significance, when people turned to read them in their context. As Michael Schmidt puts it:

> The unit of sense in a poem is not the word but the phrase or sentence a poet should consider the effect of a whole poem, not local felicities.... If not the word, then the line becomes the crucial unit, a poem is a construction made less of words than of lines, each with a dynamic which harmonises or contrasts with those that precede and follow. Rhythm, in short and long measures, displaces metre; and the appraisal of rhythm becomes a matter of nice discrimination, not a standard measurement against a yardstick (xxx).

In the twentieth century poetry and literary theory came so close that it is impossible to read poetry without theory. With the advent of the New Criticism in nineteen forties, criticism began to influence the minds of the poets. Psychoanalysis, Marxism, Deconstruction, Reader-Response Criticism, Feminism, Gender Theory and above all, Postcolonial theory continued to influence the poets and shaped their imagination. In the twentieth century poets wrote poetry by reading others' poetry. Hence, the relationship between the poet and the reader became as intimate as the two sides of the same coin. Here are two important observations by Robert Pinsky, the US Poet Laureate and T.S. Eliot respectively:

> Poetry is a vocal, which is to say a bodily, art. The medium of poetry is a human body: the column of air inside the chest, shaped into signifying sounds in the larynx and the mouth. In this sense, poetry is just as physical or bodily an art as dancing.
>
> Moreover, there is a special intimacy to poetry because, in this area of the art, the medium is not an expert's body, as when one goes to the ballet: in poetry, the medium is the audience's body (Pinsky, 8).
>
> ...poetry remains, all the same, one person talking to another; and this is just as true if you sing it, for singing is another way of talking. The immediacy of poetry to conversation is not a matter on which we can lay down exact laws. Every revolution in poetry is apt to be, and sometimes to announce itself to be, a return to common speech. That is the revolution which Wordsworth announced in his prefaces, and he was right (Eliot 23).

Louse Gluck makes the relation between the poet and the reader clear in the following words:

> When you read anything worth remembering, you liberate a human voice, you release into the world again a companion spirit. I read poems to hear that voice. And I write to speak to those I have heard. (128)

Jacques Derrida, Roland Barthes, Harold Bloom and Adrienne Rich have their own theories of poetry moving between subjectivity and objectivity. All these theories are hypothetical. If the poet is displaced from poetry, then the reader takes over. The reader brings his/her own knowledge into the poem and 'murders the poem' in order to 'dissect it'. Neither poets nor critics alone can define what poetry is. Poet critics, for whom Eliot has a word of praise in his essay, "To Criticize the Critic" closely understand the co-relation between poetry and criticism. D.H. Lawrence's statement about poetry is worth noting, says Michael Schmidt:

> He advocated a poetry of process, without goal, wedded to "the immediate present", where "there is no perfection,

> no consummation, nothing finished": open poetry, "Consummation" is a keyword, suggesting that his poems deliberately defer or avoid dramatic climax. Such climaxes set the artist outside the artifact, casting him in the role of constructor or orchestrator. For Lawrence, Whitman is the master poet of the "present", whose *Leaves of Grass* (1855) has neither beginning nor conclusion—but this, Lawrence reminds us, does not mean he has no past or future. The voice of the "present" tends to be rhapsodic, celebrating "the urgent, insurgent Now" (Schmidt XXXII).

Poetry will continue to be read, heard, recited and finally interpreted depending upon the choice of the people and the literary tradition of the place (say, country). Literary Criticism will remain forever under different canons. That bring us to a question:

What is the correlation between interpreting poetry and evaluating criticism? One analogy will make it clear. That is, interpreting poetry is like making love—each one does in his/her own way. And evaluating criticism is like following Vatsyayan's *Kamasutra* to decide which of the sixty-four arts of love making is most suitable for the purpose. To read poetry according to theory is to restrict its flavour.

WORKS CITED

Chari, V.K. "The Language of Poetry". *The Indian Journal of English Studies*, 4:1 (1963): 11-24. Print.

Cox, C.B. and A.E. Dyson. *Modern Poetry: Studies in Practical Criticism*. New Delhi: Orient Longman Ltd., 1963. Print.

Eliot, T.S. *On Poetry and Poets*. New York: Farrar, Straus and Cudahy, 1957.

——. "The Development of Yeats". *Yeats: Poems, 1919-1935. A Case Book*. Ed. Elizabeth Cullingford. London: Macmillan Press Ltd., 1984. 74-80. Print.

Gluck, Louse. *Proof and Theories*. New York: ECCO, 1995. Print.

Pinsky, Robert, *The Situation of Poetry: Contemporary Poetry and Its Traditions*. Princeton, NJ: Princeton University Press, 1976. Print.

Schmidt, Michael, ed. *The Harvill Book of Twentieth Century Poetry in English*. New Delhi: Rupa and Co., 2000. Print.

Tate, Allen. *Essays of Four Decades*. Chicago: Swallow, 1968. Print.

2

National Identity and Literary Representation in the Poetry of W.B. Yeats and Seamus Heaney

The question of identity of literature and its writers is open-ended. People enter into debates over this question arguing in favour of language, nationality and the place of domicile as the indelible mark of the identity of literature and writers. It is true that all the three—language, nationality and place of domicile—contribute in one way or the other to give an identity to literature and its writers but any one of them can't be taken as the sole criterion for this. Had language been the only criterion to decide the nomenclature of literature, the literatures written in English would be known as or 'International English Literature' (Bruce King's term and preference) but this is not the case. We have African literature, American literature, Australian literature, Canadian literature, Caribbean literature, Indian English literature, New Zealand literature and so on written in English and named after their respective countries. Hence, apart from language, nationality plays a vital role in deciding the nomenclature of literature. Added to this is the colonial, post-colonial and neo-colonial situations. Erstwhile British colonies after their independence produced literatures in English (i.e. the colonizer's language) and as the migratory movement gained momentum in the post-colonial era, many writers moved to UK and USA and wrote literature in English from there. That created problems for the identity of writers. Irish poets, W.B. Yeats and Seamus Heaney though began writing poetry with Ireland in their bones, they transcended their nationality to become a part of the British poetic tradition.

Historically Ireland became a colony of England in 1171, when Henry II came there and declared his mastery over the island. Subsequently Tudor monarchs perpetuated the colonial rule over Ireland in the Sixteenth Century C.L. Innes traces the course of colonial rule in Ireland in the following words:

> In the 1850s a secret revolutionary movement known as Fenianism gained ground among Irish emigrants in the United States, out of which the Irish Republican Brotherhood (IRB) was formed in 1873. In the 1880s, Charles Stewart Parnell was a leading figure in the campaign for self-government within the Union (Home Rule) and this was supported by the liberal government in England led by William Gladstone. Two Home Rule Bills were presented to parliament in 1886 and 1893 but both were defeated. The third Home Rule Bill was finally passed in 1914, only to be suspended because of the outbreak of World War I....
>
> In 1920 Ireland was partitioned into Northern Ireland and Southern Ireland, and with the Anglo-Irish Treaty of 1922, Southern Ireland was granted domination status and became the Irish Free State (271).

The purpose of stating the colonial status of Ireland is to say that Irish literature is part of post-colonial literature. Therefore, the homeland becomes the focus of Irish literature. The two poets W.B. Yeats (1865-1939) and Seamus Heaney (1939-2013) both Nobel Laureates, I have chosen for a study on the ground of their, rootedness to the native soil, and later on being absorbed into the English Poetic tradition. In the "Introduction" to *W.B. Yeats: Selected Poetry*, A. Norman Jeffares states Yeat's position as an Irish poet.

> His (Yeats's) aims were to write for an Irish audience and about Ireland—to re-create a specifically Irish literature. At first he drew upon the fairy and folk tales which he had heard in the West of Ireland and which he subsequently traced in printed material... He took

> an increasingly active interest in nationalist politics, at first under the influence of John O'Leary, an old Fenian leader who had spent many years in exile in Paris and later of Maud Gonne (XIII-IV).

Terrence Brown reinforces this idea in course of an article titled, "W.B. Yeats: The Tower" in the following words:

> His (Yeats's) distinction as poet and man of letters, who had contributed by his cultural work to the independence movement in his native Ireland, had received the ultimate accolade in the award of the Novel Prize for literature in December 1923. His life-long engagement in Irish Cultural Politics had also brought him to the significant office of Senator in the upper house of a new Dublin parliament, founded in 1922 after a bitter guerilla war between a volunteer Irish Republication Army and the forces of the British Crown... (Roberts 437).

W.B. Yeats knew that a poet's identity is linked with and marked by nationality. In "Under Ben Bulben" he says,

> Many times man lives and dies
> Between his two eternities.
> That of race and that of soul
> And Ancient Ireland knew it all.

No doubt, Yeats began writing poetry echoing the legends and folklore of Ireland. His early poetry "had an other-worldliness which comes from Celtic legend and a peculiar kind of simplicity derived from the folk culture of the Irish Peasants" (78) says V. de Sola Pinto, who further states that, "what is remarkable about his whole career is his sustained power of development. He could not remain a poet of Celtic Twilight" (82).

Yeats makes his stand clear from the beginning of his poetic career: "I cast my heart into my rhymes" ("To Ireland in the Coming Times") and then asserts in the same poem:

> While still I may, I write for you
> The love I lived, the dream I knew
> From our birthday, until we die

Yeats reiterated this idea in "Coole Park and Ballylee, 1931", when he writes:

> We were the last romantics—chose for theme
> Traditional sanctity and loveliness.

Yeats, 'the last romantic' matured in life and learnings and understood the plight of the old age. The poet who loved Ireland so much in the beginning of his poetic career, declared 'That's no country for old man' ('Sailing to Byzantium'). Here, I am reminded of A. Norman Jeffares' observation on the transition in Yeats's poetry:

> As his youthful ambitions were realized he saw the paradoxes of life. Irish freedom was achieved, but the glorious great houses were burnt down. Wisdom might perhaps compensate him for the loss of youth; but as his body aged his muse grew younger, 'the real man, the imagination which liveth for ever'. As a result he wrote 'The Tower' and 'Sailing to Byzantium', passionate poems of tension between the sensual and the spiritual, their unity arising out of his own complexity (xx).

It is true that Yeats began as an Irish poet but he gradually assimilated English poetic tradition and carried it further by bringing new symbols and myths into the realms of poetry. If in poems like 'Easter 1916', "Nineteen Hundred and Nineteen" and "An Irish Airman Foresees His Heath" he spoke of Irish revolution, in "Coole Park and Ballylee 1931", "The Tower" "Leda and the Swan" and "Among School Children", he clearly established the British Poetic tradition. In "Nineteen Hundred and Nineteen" he referred to the atrocity in Government and lamented:

> Man is in love and loves what vanishes
> What more is there to say?

As Andrew Sanders rightly observed:

> As an Irishman anxious to forge new loyalties, Yeats was famously detached from the British cause and British sympathies during the First World War. Unlike many of his class and religion in Ireland, he felt no moral obligation to be a combatant, nor was that obligation ever enforced by law (though conscription into the armed forces was introduced in Britain in January 1916, Ireland

> was exempted). When asked to write a war poem he later responded in a verse declaration that it was better 'in times like these/ A poet's mouth be silent'. In 'An Irish Airman Foresees His Death' he produced a particularly impressive war poem, if one that expresses an indifference to other men's cause while still indulging in an exhilaration for 'this tumult in the clouds'. From the spring of 1916 he was properly preoccupied with the consequences of the 'terrible beauty' born of the Easter Rising in Dublin and not with the interminable slaughter on the Somme or at the Ypres Salient (498).

My contention is that though Yeats began as an Irish poet and was conscious of his Irish identity, he was deeply moved by English poetry and poetic tradition beginning with Spenser through the British Romantics to the Pre-Raphaelites. Yeats was primarily concerned about himself and his own personality starting from childhood to old age, and his poetry in his life and experiences with the world—Irish and the British. In his 'General Introduction' to his works, the opening sentence of the first section titled 'The First Principle' runs like this:

> A poet writes always of his personal life, in his finest work out of his tragedy, whatever it be, remorse, lost love, or more loneliness; (qtd. in Rajan 16).

B. Rajan corroborates this view of the poet in his assessment of the poet in the following lines:

> It is unquestionable that Yeats's poetry is, nearly all of it, about himself, it is also unquestionable that it is about a great deal more. The best of his work bears most strongly his individual stamp but it is also impersonal because it is a whole, creating its own *raison d'etre* and logic (17).

Yeats's poetry, as many critics take it, is an embodiment of sustained growth and development. But I think, Yeats's early poetry deeply soaked in romanticism and love for his country Ireland (it may be mentioned here that he founded Irish Academy of Letters to promote young Irish authors) gradually yielded place to realism and spirituality—may be seeking eternity for the redemption of mankind. A Norman Jeffares makes an important observation in the following words:

> Thus, by the time of his marriage, in 1917 when he was fifty-two, he had experienced the heights and depths of public life, just as his poetry had swung from a romantic extreme to a realistic. And then, almost miraculously, came the sudden great flowering, for now Yeats began the new, exciting poetry, founded, in part, upon the ideas he included in his book *A Vision* with its vistas of history, its views of man and of the supernatural, and in part upon the reflections he based upon the experiences of his own life. His poetry could now include beauty and realism, and magically he fused these extremes into emotive rhetoric. He could use both self and soul in one poem and compel them into a unity, of the whole man, of the poetic personality (*The Circus Animals* 23).

This view of Jeffares is corroborated by V. de S. Pinto in his well-known book, *Crisis in English Poetry 1880-1940.* Pinto observes:

> 'Sailing to Byzantium' (1920) should be read in conjunction with its sequel, 'Byzantium', written four years later. The first poem is a picture of a voyage from the material world to the holy city of eternity; the second is a vision of the city from the inside where the soul is imaged first as a walking mummy and then as the Emperor's golden bird, whose 'glory of changeless metal' is contrasted with the 'complexities of mire and blood'. Here Byzantium is a Purgatory as well as a Paradise, a place of cleansing flames (95).

Seamus Heaney, W.B. Yeats's great successor ironically was born in the year of the death of the latter. Robert Lowell calls him, 'the most important Irish poet since Yeats'. If Yeats began writing poetry being influenced by Spenser, Shelley and the Pre-Raphaelites, Heaney appreciated Wordsworth during his childhood, later in life he read and was moved by the poetry of Hopkins, Robert Frost and W.B. Yeats. Like T.S. Eliot, Seamus Heaney is a well read person. As a poet, dramatist and translator,

Heaney has assimilated all his learning which later on went into to making his own poetry. Dominic Alapat makes an apt observation in this regard in the following words:

> Robert Frost with his native witticisms, William Yeats with his passion and theory of Irish history and the universe, Patrick Kavanagh with his picturesque rural simplicity, Ted Hughes' poems about the primality of man and his world, Thomas Hardy's melancholic elegies, the entire English literary tradition, Wilfred Owen's poems appealing to mankind about the destruction of war and who was killed in the trenches of WW I, all influenced his poetic sensibility. Seamus Heaney read and inculcated these poems in his own way (97).

He was conscious of his personal memories and national history which helped him to take his decision to write poetry deviating from the family tradition of potato-digging. He makes it evident in a poem called, "Digging".

> The cold smell potato mould, the squelch and sap
> Of soggy peat, the curt cuts of an edge
> Through living roots awaken in my hand
> But I've no spade to follow men like them.
>   Between my finger and my thumb
>   The squat pen rests
>   I'll dig with it.

Andrew Sanders traces the origin of Heaney as a man and poet to the latter's lecture in 1976:

> In a lecture given in 1976, and reprinted in his collection of essays *Pre-occupations* (1980), the Irish poet Seamus Heaney (b.1939) traced a 'defensive love of their territory' which was once shared only by those poets whom we might call colonial. Heaney counts himself amongst the colonials, but, as other essays in the volume suggest, he is fully aware of the doubleness and division of his inheritance.
>
> 'I speak and write in English', he noted in an article written in 1972, 'but do not altogether share the preoccupations and perspectives of an Englishman...the

> English tradition is not ultimately home. I live off another hump as well.' That other 'hump' is the Ireland, or more particularly the rural Ulster, which figures so delicately, richly and painfully in his verse. His Irish inheritance is multiple (608).
>
> The titles of Heaney's books of verse include *Death of a Naturalist* (1966), *Door into the Dark* (1969), *Wintering Out* (1972), *North* (1975), *Filed Work* (1979), *Station Island* (1984), *The Haw Lantern* (1987), *Seeing Things* (1991) and *The Spirit Level* (1996). Of all these volumes *North* is considered to be the hallmark in his poetic career. It is about Northern Island and its various problems. In the words of Dominic Alapat, "This collection, also Heaney's darkest, has poems about local killings and funerals and the people's attempts to come to terms with them. It contains several of the 'Bog' poems like "Viking Dublin: Trial Pieces", "The Garuballe Man", "Punishment", etc. It also includes the brilliant "Singing School", a set of six poems'...(98).

In course of an article titled, "Representation in Modern Irish Poetry", Eamonn Hughes writes:

> The second section of Seamus Heaney's *North* particularly 'Singing School', is a pivotal moment in his career. Although often dismissed, it is Heaney's first sustained interrogation of his intimacy with English Culture. His response is to strip his writing of the influences of that culture. His later writing shows this to have been a wrong turning, rejects the attempted nativism of 'Singling School' and returns to English culture with a new and dialectical purpose... (Allen 78).

Heaney carried forward Yeats's attempt of bringing politics centre—stage as a theme in a poem called, "Mediations in Time of Civil War" in his book of poems, *North*. "If the poetry's public concerns and its concentration of symbols are what makes *North* an outstanding book, the refusal of this poem, to take refuse from judgement makes this the most important single poems", says Bernard O'Donoghue (Roberts 534).

In his "Review of Fieldwork" Terry Eagleton tells us that it is inappropriate to compare Seamus Heaney, a Northern Ireland catholic poet to W.B. Yeats, a Southern Ireland protestant poet simply because both of them are Irishman.

> There are two particular reasons, among thousand of others why the comparison of Heaney with Yeats is inept. Yeats's conception of poetry was a fairly common place. Romantic inspirationalism entailing an irrationalism not unconnected with his politics. Hedaney by contrast, conceives art as analogous to manual labour, a traffic with Nature mediated by verbal rather than material instruments (Allen 102).

Eagleton is unnecessarily harsh to W.B. Yeats in his desire to elevate Heaney to a superior position. He over looks the last stanza of "Among School Children" where Yeats speaks of art as the product of labour and the separation of art and artist is impossible. However, Terry Eagleton is right when he says that Heaney, 'probably is one of the finest English—language poets of the Century' (Allen 105).

Both Yeats and Heaney brought violence and power to the realms of poetry. If Heaney says, 'with time to kill/ They are taking their time' in "Mossbawn: Two Poems in Dedication", in "The Harvest Bow" he asserts, "The end of art is peace". W.B. Yeats takes a detached view in "An Irish Airman Foresees His Death" and writes:

> Those that I fight I do not hate
> Those that I guard I don't love...
> I balanced all, brought all to mind.

The question of identity of a poet is linked with nationality and language. Sometimes the language in which a poet writes may not be his national language and he may be inspired by the poets of the language in which he writes. It is in this case, that the poet has to bring a correlation between his nationality and the language he writes in by accepting both and rejecting neither. Here I would like to refer to an observation made by Irish nationalist critics, D.F. MacCarthy in the edited book, *The Book of Irish Ballads* to clarify the position of the poet:

> ...that we can be thoroughly Irish in our feelings without ceasing to be English in our speech; that we can be faithful to the land of our birth, without being ungrateful to that literature which has been 'the nursing mother of our minds'; that we can develop the intellectual resources of our country, and establish for ourselves a distinct and separate existence in the world of letters without depriving ourselves of the advantages of the widely-diffused and genius-consecrated language of England, are facts that I conceive cannot be too widely disseminated (qtd. in Lloyd), (Allen 157).

Yeats and Heaney have been evaluated by critics as poles apart on romantic and realistic binary scale, and yet they are an integral part of Irish poetic tradition. If Yeats brings politics centre-stage in "Meditations in Time of Civil War", in the Deane interview Heaney concedes having given a thought to politics in his poetry. Heaney says,

> I always thought of the political problem—may be because I am not really a political thinker—as being an internal Northern Ireland division. I thought along sectarian lines. Now I think that the genuine political confrontation is between Ireland and Britain (*The Crane Bag* 62-63).

Both Yeats and Heaney belong to the Irish tradition but they have transformed it by their individual talent. What is common to both of them is the transcendence of native tradition and assimilation of British tradition in their poetry. In "Contemporary Irish Poetry", Lucy Collins writes:

> Heaney is a poet who embodies the modern need to explore national mythologies in an international poetic context. His preoccupation with his origins remains strong and his use of rural tradition at once evokes the sensual immediacy of childhood and probes the implications of literary tradition itself. The combination of consummate craftsmanship and intuitive handling of subtle emotional territories links Heaney's poetic process with his key themes; this suggestive interweaving

is accompanied by a range of poetic influences from Dante to Robert Lowell. Heaney's attention to the Gaelic heritage also suggests the necessity of mediating between traditions (Roberts 588).

What Anna Swir, the Polish poet says about the making of a poet applies to both Yeats and Heaney equally well. If as Swir points that, "a poet becomes an antenna capturing the voices of the world, a medium expressing his own subconscious and the collective subconscious" (qtd. in Heaney, Allen 131), Yeats and Heaney have proved the point.

To conclude, I should say that both Yeats and Heaney though belonged to Ireland and began their poetic career as Irish poets, they have been fully absorbed into English poetic tradition and contributed immensely to Modern English Poetry. Their poetry brings Ireland and Britain close and blurred the line between the colonized and colonizer. They didn't write back to the centre but write with the centre. There in lies the strength and authenticity of their poetry. Their literary representation transcended national identity.

WORKS CITED

Alapat, Dominic. "Souns from the Irish Bog". *Gentleman.* 21:1 (January, 2001): 97-99. Print.

Brown, Terence. "W.B. Yeats: The Tower". *A Companion to Twentieth-Century Poetry.* Ed. Neil Roberts. Melbourne: Blackwell Publishing Ltd., 2003. Print.

Collins, Lucy. "Contemporary Irish Poetry". *A Companion to Twentieth-Century Poetry.* Ed. Neil Roberts. Melbourne: Blackwell Publishing Ltd., 2003. Print.

Eagleton, Terry. "Review of Fieldwork". *Seamus Heaney.* Ed. Michael Allen. London: MacMillan, 1992. Print.

Heaney, Seamus. "The Government of the Tongue". *Seamus Heaney.* Ed. Michael Allen. London: MacMillan Press Ltd., 1977: 129-46. Print.

Hughes, Eamonn. "Representation in Modern Irish Poetry". *Seamus Heaney.* Ed. Michael Allen. London: MacMillan, 1997. Print.

Innes, C.L. *The Cambridge Introduction to Postcolonial Literatures in English,* New Delhi: Cambridge University Press, 2007. Print.

Jeffares, A. Norman. *W.B. Yeats: Selected Poetry.* London: MacMillan, 1972. Print.

Jeffares, A. Norman. *The Circus Animals: Essays on W.B. Yeats*. London: MacMillan, 1970. Print.

Lloyd, David. "Pap for the Dispossessed: Seamus Heaney and the Poetics of Identity". *Seamus Heaney.* Ed. Michael Allen. London: MacMillan, 1997. Print.

O'Donoghue, Bernard. "Seamus Heaney: North". *A Companion to Twentieth-Century Poetry.* Ed. Neil Roberts. Melbourne: Blackwell Publishing Ltd., 2003. Print.

Pinto, V. de S. *Crisis in English Poetry 1880-1940.* London: Hubchinson and Co., 1967. Print.

Rajan, Balachandra, *W.B. Yeats: A Critical Introduction.* London: Hulchinson and Co., 1972. Print.

Sanders, Andrew. *The Short Oxford History of English Literature.* Oxford: Clarendon Press, 1996. Print.

3

T.S. Eliot and Nissim Ezekiel: The Making of the Poetic Canon

T.S. Eliot and Nissim Ezekiel have been hailed as the liberators of Modern English poetry and Indian English poetry from the traditional verse of their own countries. American born British poet, Eliot revolutionalized English poetry by bringing anthropology, psychology, philosophy, metaphysics, European and Indian myths into the realms of it. Together with Ezra Pound, Eliot popularized imagist movement in English poetry. If Eliot, who spoke of tradition, moved away from it, Ezekiel sought to liberate modern Indian English poetry from Anglo-American influence by emphasizing geography and landscape of the country instead of history. This chapter seeks to highlight the contributions of Eliot and Ezekiel to modern poetry of their respective countries which went a long way in establishing the poetic canon.

The paralysed human mind failing to choose between the conscious and subconscious state resulting in the failure of love, is aptly conveyed by a startling image, 'like a patient etherised upon the table' in the opening lines of "The Love Song of J. Alfred Prufrock". Here is a love song which remains unsung. And yet, the hope is not abandoned, for, "In a minute there is time/ For decisions and revisions which a minute will reverse".

Eliot dives deep into history and observes that "History has many cunning passages, contrived corridors" ("Gerontion"). V. de S. Pinto makes an apt observation in the following lines:

> Eliot had the advantage of being brought up in the tradition of English literary culture, and yet, at the same time, of being able to see it, as a foreigner sees it, from the outside. It was an advantage which could, perhaps, be only fully enjoyed by an American with a cosmopolitan education. One the other hand, his early life in America brought him into touch with a society which was probably even more corrupt and hostile to spiritual values than that of Europe. This was a disadvantage, because he thus acquired an excessive preoccupation with the stateness and flatness of modern life, as well as a kind of fastidious shrinking from its brutality and meanness, which colours much of his poetry (143).

Eliot's early poetry describes 'the boredoms, the horror and the glory' (*The Use of Poetry and the Use of Criticism*) of the modern world, which culminates in *The Waste Land* (1922). In this epoch making poem, Eliot makes use of psychology, anthropology and myths to establish a pattern. The burden of the poem is how to create a myth that would give expression to a morally bankrupt society shattered by the World War I. V. de S. Pinto observes:

> For this purpose Eliot makes use of the two typically modern sciences of psychology and anthropology. Translations of the writing of Sigmund Freud had attracted widespread interest in psycho-analysis and the psychology of sex in the years immediately following the First World War, and they had already exercised considerable influence on writers such as James Joyce and D.H. Lawrence. The central conception of *The Waste Land* is sexual impotence used as a symbol for the spiritual malady of the modern world. This symbol is developed by means of a myth which had been much studied by contemporary anthropologists. This is the vegetation myth with the rites of fertility based upon it found in the Eastern cults described by Sir James Frazer in his *Attis, Adonis, Osiris* (1920), to which Eliot acknowledges a particular debt. The specific example of the myth which he selects is derived from the theory of Miss J.L. Weston, expounded in several of her

> books and notably in *From Ritual to Romance* (1920). Miss Weston's theory was that the story of the quest for the Holy Grail was a Christianised version of 'an ancient Ritual, having for its ultimate objects the initiation into the secret of the Sources of Life, physical and Spiritual, in fact a ritual based on a vegetation myth of the same kind as the myth of Adonis and similar Eastern cults (151-52).

This poem is an much a tribute to his scholarship as to his craftsmanship. "It is amazing how with London base the poem radiates in time and space to Greek, Roman, Phoemician Egyptian and Indian civilizations and from there to the cosmic heights where once gods demons and men heard what the Thunder said and their progeny must now hear in their deep hearts core—if they have followed the poem" (Narasimhaiah 38).

Eliot visualized a waste land. This land may be anywhere and it can exist at any point of time. He introduced the fertility rites and the celebrations of a renewed life. In his Memorial Lecture of W.B. Yeats, Eliot says that the great poet is the man who, "out of intense and personal experience is able to express a general truth: retaining all the particularity of his experience to make of it a general symbol". This is what he does in *The Waste Land.* He 'connects nothing with nothing' and asks, "Shall I at least set my lands in order?" Sisir Kumar Ghose makes an important observation on the poem in the following lines:

> It is impossible not to admire in this poem of romantic agony and ennui, "the strange deadly poem" of a young poet on the verge of nervous breakdown, measuring immeasurable, invisible losses, the sheer honesty of experience, and sense of shared guilt; it is these that would not allow either any slick solution or an elegiac *sic transit gloria mundi.* ("so passes the glory of the world") (*Span* 36).

Eliot continued to write about the decadent aspect of life for three more years after *The Waste Land* (i.e., upto *The Hollow Men* 1925). Modern humanity is perceived a 'stuffed men' with 'headpiece filled with straw'. No wonder, they fail to see the truth and comprehend reality, and hence for them,

> Between the idea
> And the reality
> Between the motion
> And the act
> Falls the Shadow ("The Hollow Men")

The poem comes to a close with a famous stanza, tinged with irony which explains the helplessness of Western Europe in the second decade of the twentieth century and after.

> This is the way the world ends
> This is the way the world ends
> This is the way the world ends
> Not with a bang but a whimper (Jain 72).

Eliot's poetry has undergone transformation after his conversation to Anglo-Catholocism in 1927. The early phase of his poetry beginning with "The Love Song of J. Alfred Prufrock" and ending with "The Hollow Men" which portrayed the 'boredom and horror' of life embodied in the declining values of life devoid of 'glory', has now yielded place to an acceptance of life through surrender "Our peace in His will" (*Ash-Wednesday* line 214). The search for meaning in life prompted the poet to look within and pine for what has been lost in our ignorance. Eliot asks:

> Where is the Life we have lost in living?
> Where is the wisdom we have lost in knowledge?
> Where is the knowledge we have lost in information?
> (Choruses from 'The Rock' lines 14-16).

By the time Eliot wrote "Choruses for 'The Rock' (1934) and *Four Quartets* (1939-1942 collected edition 1943), "Christ the Tiger" (Gerontion) has become 'the wounded surgeon' (East Coker), 'who remembers the way to your door'. V. de S. Pinto makes a perceptive comment on the design and substance of *Four Quartets* in the following lines:

> The subject had already been hinted at in the fourth section of *Ash Wednesday*. It is time, its relation to the timeless and the 'redemption' of time. Two fragments of the early Greek philosopher Herakleitos are quoted on the title page. One suggests the famous Heraclitean

> doctrine of flux, the constant interchange between the four elements of air, earth, water, and fire between life and death, This interchange can be regarded as a 'way up', but, since according to Herakleitos it is a cyclic movement, it can equally be regarded as a 'way down'. The other fragment refers to Herakleitos's doctrine of the logos or directive intelligence behind the eternal flux, an intelligence with which human reason and language is connected. This doctrine has an obvious affinity to Christian teaching (161).

In "Burnt Norton" Eliot speaks of "other echoes/ Inhabit the garden. Shall we follow?" That is why, he dived deep into his own culture (all the four poems of *Four Quartets* are named after four places connected with Eliot's ancestry and memory), and then looked to the French symbolists for inspiration, and then learned Sanskrit and Pali to imbibe the wisdom of the East. In "Tradition and the Individual Talent" he says the "the whole of the literature of Europe from Homer and within it the whole of the literature of his own country has a simultaneous existence and composes a simultaneous order" and that is, what he exemplifies in his own poetry. C.D. Narasimhaiah makes an apt observation on this aspect of Eliot's poetry in the following words:

> The poet's business, he intimates in *Four Quartets,* was only to recover what had been discovered once or twice and lost and found again, by men who knew better—an attitude which reinforced his profoundly felt humility. But religion and poetry had seldom come so close in any poem in living memory as here (37-38).

Eliot writes:

> Do not let me hear
> Of the wisdom of old men, but rather of their folly...
> The only wisdom we can hope to acquire
> Is the wisdom of humility: humility is endless.
>
> (East Coker)

In his Nobel Prize acceptance speech Eliot says,

> When a poet speaks to his own people, the voices of all the poets of other languages who have influenced him are

> speaking also. And at the same time he himself is speaking to younger poets of other languages, and these poets will convey something of his vision of life and something of the spirit of his people, to their own. Partly through his influence on other poets, partly through readers of his language who are not themselves poets, the poet can contribute towards understanding between peoples (qtd. in Das 64).

Jesus and Krishna have taken a section each ("East Coker IV" and "Dry Salvages III") in which Eliot reminds us of "Adam's curse/ And that, to be restored, our sickness must grow worse" and Krishna's admonition of Arjun, "On the field of battle/ Not farewell,/ But fare forward, Voyagers". No wonder, Eliot understands that "right action is freedom/ From past and future also", and comes to the conclusion that all religion is one religion. Hence, he concludes the poem wishing mankind well:

> And all shall be well and
> All manner of thing shall be well
> When the tongues of flame are in-folded
> Into the crowned knot of fire
> And the fire and rose are one.
> ("Little Gidding")

Nissim Ezekiel (1924-2004) is conscious artist, who sought to overcome the imitative phase of pre-Independence Indian English Poetry, by focusing on contemporary life. No wonder, his first book of verse was published with a significant title, *A Time to Change* (1952). If "words, looks, gestures, everything betrays/ The unquiet mind, the emptiness within", the poet becomes conscious of his identity. Hence comes the resolution:

> I cannot leave the island.
>
> I was born here and belong.
> (Island)

The poet has to make his commitments now, 'This is one: to stay where I am'. Following Eliot and Auden, Ezekiel wrote about the Modern City which 'like a passion burns'. Bombay has become a 'Barbaric City sick with slums'. If for Eliot, "Home is where one starts from" ('East Coker') for Ezekiel, "Home is where we have to gather grace".

Eliot and Ezekiel have something in common—that is, both of them brought everyday conversational language into the realms of poetry. If for Eliot, the poet is involved 'with the intolerable wrestle/with words and meanings', for Ezekiel, 'the best poets wait forwards'. Poems like "Night of the Scorpion", "Enterprise", "Poet, Lover, Birdwatcher". "The Professor" and "Very 'Indian' Poems in Indian English" bring conversational language into the realms of poetry. Irony and parody became favourite mode in Ezekiel's poetry.

In "The Professor" Ezekiel says,

These are days of family planning.
I am not against. We have to change with times.
Whole world is changing. In India also
We are keeping up. Our progress is progressing.
Old values are going, new values are coming.
Everything is happening with leaps and bounds. (*CP* 239)

The irony is unmistakable. In "Hangover", Ezekiel observes:

The foreigners and the foreign—returned.
The expensive menu and the shadow of Marx.
The Biryani Hyderabadi and the sighs for Bangla Desh.
The see—through dress and the show—nothing sari.
The fog in the head and the sense of success.
The music Indian and the language English. (*CP* 233)

Like Eliot, Ezekiel also goes to the roots to rediscover the past ad writes a cycle of poem called, "Passion Poems" and another called "Nudes 1978" following the ancient Sanskrit poets. Let me cite two short poems from "Passion Poems" and one from "Nudes 1978" to drive home the points:

How freely they mention
breasts and buttocks.
They are my poetic ancestors.
Why am I so inhibited? ("The Sanskrit Poems", *CP* 214)

Krishna's tricks
are not for him

> nor Radha's wiles
> for her.
> They have a different truth
> within a kingdom of their own.
> I envy them. ("A Marriage", *CP* 215)

> Artist of the nude
> who cannot draw,
> fears the camera,
> will not contemplate
> for long, either art
> or pornography, must
> resort to something
> more direct—desire
> dared, sent forth Zen-eyed
> to bring her in, saying,
> 'Yes, this is me as I am,'
> naked seen, seeing nakedness,
> named flawed in detail,
> womanly and vulnerable. ("Nudes 1978 XIV", *CP* 252)

If Eliot lays emphasis on the consummation of love for procreation in *The Waste Land* against the degeneration of it into lust in the case of the typist girl and the lover, Ezekiel depicts the disastrous consequences of love in "Case Study" and "Jewish Wedding in Bombay". "His marriage was the worst mistake of all" because, "A man is damned in that domestic game" says Ezekiel in "Case Study". The gender bias becomes obvious. In "Jewish Wedding in Bombay" Ezekiel makes amends by stating that if marriage fails it is the woman who is the worst sufferer. The poem concludes:

> During our first serious marriage quarrel she said Why did you take my virginity from me? I would gladly have returned it, but not one of the books I had read instructed me how (*CP* 235).

Like Eliot, Ezekiel has also studied Philosophy and wrote some poems in the manner of Eliot's 'Choruses from *the Rock*' and *Four Quartets,* though Ezekiel can't by any stretch of imagination equal Eliot's achievement. Ezekiel's 'Hymns in

Darkness' and "Latter—Day Psalms" are philosophical poems in which Ezekiel celebrates spirit as a preference to matter. Here are a few examples:

He has lost faith in himself
and found faith at last. ("Hymns in Darkness")
The darkness has its secrets
Which light does not know. ("Hymns in Darkness")
For the Lord only knows how the
way to him is found ("Latter—Day Psalms")
Except the Lord build the house
and not even always then—
they labour in vain that build
it.
("Latter—Day Psalms")

This reminds us of Eliot's lines 'We only live, only suspire/ consumed by either fire or fire.' ("Little Gidding")

Eliot and Ezekiel have influenced poets who succeeded them. Eliot's influence is international but Ezekiel's is national. Jayanta Mahapatra, Keki N. Daruwalla, Dom Moraes, Shiv K. Kumar—all acknowledge their indebtedness to Ezekiel. In course of an interview given to me (*The Critical Endeavour* Vol. XVII, Jan. 2011) Keki N. Daruwalla acknowledges Nissim Ezekiel's greatness as a poet and humanist. Both Eliot and Ezekiel began as poets who looked life from negative point of view, finally ended as great humanistic poets. They fashioned a new vocabulary for poetry and set the taste for the age. Eliot and Ezekiel brought the readers of their own countries close to poetry. This is a significant achievement by any standard, anywhere in the world.

To a question, 'What makes an author canonical'? Harold Bloom says, "The answer, more often than not, has turned out to be strangeness, a mode of originality that either cannot be assimilated or that so assimilates us that we cease to see it as strange" (3).

Now the greatness in English poetry and Indian English poetry centres upon Eliot and Ezekiel respectively. "Canonical prophecy needs to be tested about two generations after a writer dies" (522) says Harold Bloom. Eliot has fulfilled this and Ezekiel, one hopes will do so in the future.

WORKS CITED

Bloom, Harold. *The Western Canon.* London: MacMillan 1995. Print.

Das, Bijay Kumar. "The Importance of T.S. Eliot", *The Heritage.* 4:12, 1988, 62-65. Print.

Eliot, T.S. *Four Quartets.* Delhi: OUP, 1977. Print.

Ezekiel, Nissim. *Collected Poems.* Delhi: OUP, 2009. Print.

Ghose, Sisir Kumar. "*The Waste Land* Revisited". *Span.* (July 1981). 33-39. Print.

Jain, Manju, ed. *Selected Poems and A Critical Readings of the Selected Poems of T.S. Eliot.* Delhi: OUP, 1996. Print.

Narasimhaiah, C.D. "*The Waste Land* Vindicated". *Span.* (July 1981). 33-39. Print.

Pinto, V. de S. *Crisis in English Poetry.* London: Hutchinson & Co (Publishers) Ltd., 1967. Print.

4

Post-1950 Indian English Poetry: The Making of a Canon

Indian English poetry has moved a long way since Nissim Ezekiel published his first book of verse, *A Time to Change* (1952) in London. Sixty-two years in the life of Indian English poetry is a long time to form a canon in Indian English literature. Some of the poems by Indian English poets have gained international recognition and found their way to several anthologies both at home and abroad. This brings to our mind the question of what makes a canon.

It is relevant to refer to Harold Bloom's well-known book, *The Western Canon.* He ponders over the question, 'What makes the author and the works canonical' and says, "the answer more often than not, has turned out to be strangeness, a mode of originality that either cannot be assimilated or that so assimilates us that we cease to see it as strange" (Bloom 3). He further states that, "One mark of an originality that can win canonical status for a literary work is a strangeness that we either never altogether assimilate, or that becomes such a given that we are blinded to its idiosyncrasies. Dante is the largest instance of the first possibility, and Shakespeare, the overwhelming example of the second" (4).

What I propose to do in course of this chapter is to focus not on the poets as such but on the poems which have gained acceptance by the academics as well as the reading public. Secondly, I want to apply critical theories such as Reader-Response criticism, Feminist criticism, New Historicism and Post Colonial criticism to the canonical poems. Before taking the poems for a close analysis let me briefly make a diachronic study of it. In the introduction to my book, *New Readings in Indian English Literature*, I have made the following observations:

> Post-independence era (we may say post-colonial period) witnessed the rise of Indian English poets who wrote a substantial body of Indian English poetry that won national and international recognition. The leader of the post-independence poetic movement was Nissim Ezekiel, a 'founding father' (Bruce King's coinage) of Indian English poetry. Poets like Nissim Ezekiel, Kamala Das, A.K. Ramanujan, Dom Moraes, R. Parthasarathy, Jayanta Mahapatra, Shiv K. Kumar, Keki N. Daruwalla, Adil Jusswalla, A.K. Mehrotra, Arun Kolatkar, P. Lal, Pritish Nandy, O.P. Bhatnagar, Eunice Desouza, Mamta Kalia, Gauri Deshpande, Meena Alexander and a host of others dominated the Indian English poetry from 1960s to 1980s. They have outgrown Anglo-American influence and produced a distinct body of Indian English poetry with made in Indian stamp on it.
>
> If P. Lal espoused the cause of Indian English poetry by establishing Writers Workshop in Calcutta in 1958, R. Parthasarathy accentuated the growth of it in mid 1970s. As the poetry editor of the Oxford University Press, New Delhi, he has published his epoch making book, *Ten Twentieth Century Indian Poets* (1976) and the books of verse by Ezekiel, Daruwalla, Shiv K. Kumar and a host of others. (Ramanujan has published his books of verse by OUP much before). Ezekiel's *Hymns in Darkness* (1976), *Latter—Day Psalm* (1982), Daruwalla's *Crossing of Rivers* (1976). *The Keeper of the Dead* (1982), Ramanujan's *Selected Poems* (1977), Parthasarathy's *Rough Passage* (1976), Shiv K. Kumar's *Subterfuges* (1977) and Jayanta Mahapatra's *Selected Poems* (1987) are milestones in Indian English poetry. Indian English poetry shows two distinct trends in the post-independence period. One group of poets led by Ezekiel sought to identify themselves with contemporary

> India—people, places and society. They wrote in the ironic mode. Ezekiel's *Hymns in Darkness* and *Latter—Day Psalms* are master texts in this direction. The other group of poets led by A.K. Ramanujan, and Kamala Das, turned inward and sought to evoke tradition, history and culture of the land in English language. Jayanta Mahapatra won international recognition by winning prizes and publishing in prestigious poetry journals/ magazines like *Critical Quarterly, The Sewanee Review, the Hudson Review and Kenyon Review,* abroad. Ezekiel, Ramanujan, Parthasarathy, Daruwalla and Kumar too published abroad. Younger generation of poets like Meena Alexander, Bibhu Padhi, Sujata Bhatt, Shanta Acharya and a few others too have published abroad. Indian English poetry now stands on its own ground and is read favourably with poetry written in English elsewhere in the world outside Anglo-American tradition (2-3).

Indian English poets belong to three categories—one, those who write in English and live in India like Bibhu Padhi, Keki N. Daruwalla, Jayanta Mahapatra and many others, two, those who write in English but live in foreign countries like Meena Alexandar, Shanta Acharya, Sujata Bhatt and a few others, three, those who write in English and divide their time between India and abroad like R. Parthasarathy, Vikram Seth, Shiv K. Kumar and a few others. Some of our well known and pioneering poets like Nissim Ezekiel, Kamala Das Dom Moraes, A.K. Ramanujan and P. Lal are no more with us.

Nissim Ezekiel, A.K. Ramanujan, Kamala Das, R. Parthasarathy, Jayanta Mahapatra, Adil Jusswalla, Shiv K. Kumar, Keki N. Daruwalla, Dom Moraes, Arun Kolatkar, A.K. Mehrotra, P. Lal, Pritish Nandy who wrote between 1950 and 1990, produced some of the remarkable poems. Most of these well-known poets have won Sahitya Akademi Awards and brought out collections of their poems under the title, *Collected Poems*. These include Nissim Ezekiel's *Collected Poems 1952-1988* (OUP, 1989), A.K. Ramanujan's *The Collected Poems of A.K. Ramanujan* (OUP, 1999), Keki N. Daruwalla's *Collected*

Poems 1970-2005 (Penguin Books 2006), Dom Moraes's *Collected Poems 1954-2004* (Penguin Books, 2004), Kamala Das's *Collected Poems* Vol. 1 (1984) and *Only the Soul Knows How to Sing* (DC Books 1996), Jayanta Mahapatra's, *Selected Poems* (OUP 1982) and *The Life of Dawns, 1974-2008* (Authors Press, 2009). The eight poets who won the Sahitya Akademi Award are Jayanta Mahapatra for *Relationship* (1981), Nissim Ezekiel for *Latter—Day Psalms* (1983), Keki N. Daruwalla for *The Keeper of the Dead* (1984), Kamala Das for *Collected Poems* Vol. 1 (1985), Shiv K. Kumar for *Trapfalls in the Sky* (1987), Dom Moraes for *Serendip* (1994), A.K. Ramanujan for *The Collected Poems of A.K. Ramanujan* (1999), and Jeet Thayil for *These Errors are Correct* (2012).

The poems that have attained canonical status are Jayanta Mahapatra's *Relationship,* "A Country", "The Lost Children of America", "A Pastoral Perhaps", "The Abandoned British Cemetry at Balasore", and "Hunger", Nissim Ezekiel's "Night of the Scorpion", "Jewish Wedding in Bombay", "Nudes 1978", "Hymns in Darkness", "Poet Lover, Birdwatcher", "Background, Casually", "The Visitor" and "In India", A.K. Ramanujan's "A River", "Small Scale Reflections on a Great House", "Second Sight", "Love Poem for Wife 1", "Some Indian Uses of History on a Rainy Doy", Keki N. Daruwalla's "The Ghaghra in Spate", "Crossing of Rivers", "Death of a Bird", "Migrations", "The Parsi Hell", "The Hebrew Professor", Dom Moraes's, "Landscape", "Painter", "Homo Sapiens", "Myth", Kamala Das's "An Introduction", "The Looking Glass", "Home is a Concept", "Blood", "Substitute", Shiv K. Kumar's "Lord Krishna to Arjuna", "Twenty-fifth Wedding Anniversary", "I say it on Oath, your Lordship", R. Parthasarathy's "Exile" and "Home Coming", Bibhu Padhi's "House Lizards", "Portrait of a Family" Niranjan Mohanty's long poem, "Prayer to Lord Jagannath", Shanta Acharya's "Highgate Cemetry", Makrand Paranjape's "Torsos" and "The Homecoming" and a few other poems by twenty-first century poets such as Tabis Khair, Leela Gandhi, Ranjit Hoskote, Rabindra K. Swain, Gopi Krishnan Kottoor, C.P. Surendran, Anita Nair and Robin S. Ngangom.

Indian English poetry in the last sixty-two years (1952-2014) has taken two routes: One, diving deep into history, culture and tradition of the nation, and two, moving on the surface depicting landscape, places and people of the country. To the first category belong Jayanta Mahapatra, A.K. Ramanujan, Kamala Das, R. Parthasarathy, Shiv K. Kumar, Arun Kolatkar and to the second category belong Nissim Ezekiel, Keki N. Daruwalla, Adil Jusswalla, and a few other poets. Its time that brings a qualitative change in Indian English poetry.

The first thing that strikes us in Modern Indian English Poetry is the narration of the nation in clear cut terms. Love, death, time, disappointments, failures in contemporary society, attract the attention of the poets. They see life steadily and see it whole.

I would like to make an explication of some of the canonical poems and begin with Jayanta Mahapatra's *Relationship*. In course of an article titled "The Inaudible Resonance in English Poetry in India", Jayanta Mahapatra Writes:

> *Relationship* is a product of dreams, has made me speak of the demands of a pilgrimage—a pilgrimage threatened by the living Oriya past, by nagging hunger and a persistent sexuality. (*The Literary Criterion* 36)

Let me approach this poem from the angle of New historicism First I would re-situate the text in the context and then examine the historicity of the text by reconfiguring textuality and history.

The heroic Oriya past is vividly remembered and recalled with a sense of nostalgia. The glory and pride of our ancestors exhibited in the climactic Kalinga War in 261 B.C. which turned Ashok the Great into a deeply religious man, is now a long lost trait in our racial character. The river Daya is a witness to our ancestor's heroic effort which has become a sort of myth for us. Once heroic and militant race is no more than mere memory now for its successors proved to be unworthy of keeping the glory of their ancestors afloat and drifted away from their ideals. Thus, Mahapatra notices a sharp contrast in the descending order between the past and the present marking an overwhelming decline in values of life in our time.

The poet's life is integrated with the heroic tradition of the land of his birth and as he becomes conscious of it, his heart throbs and a kind of unknown fear engulfs him. The landscape of Odisha moves him when he observes the annual migrating birds from far north Siberia to the warm waters of Chilika, a beautiful lake in Orissa. The agony of the poet springs from the fact that while the birds and animals react naturally to the seasons of the year, he is cut off as it were from the heroic traditions of his ancestors. He tells that 'I can never come alive/ if I refuse to consecrate at the altar of my origins' and thus 'a prayer to draw my body out of a thousand years'. There is a sense of nostalgia which pervades the atmosphere of the poem. Cuttack, a city of historical importance, which had the great Barabati Fort, is now a symbol of 'vanquished dynasties'. A sense of belonging overwhelms the poet and in a voice charged with emotion he tells us:

> Now I stand among these ruins,
> waiting for the cry of a night bird
> from the river's far side
> to drift through my weariness
> listening to the voices of my friends
> who have become the friends of others,
> writing poems, abject and anxious
> in rooms which reek of old folk,
> of their sloth and arthritis and neglect,
> like state cupboards which are going black
> with the smells of the rancid fat of the past.
>
> (*Relationship* 35)

There seems to be a need for pilgrimage to the 'Living Oriya Past' in order to recognize the present and lead a meaningful life by imbibing spirit of the glorious past and tradition of the land. Like W.B. Yeats's "Leda and the Swan", *Relationship* is an amalgam of history, myth and vision.

We can apply formalistic criticism by taking irony as a dominant mode to Nissim Ezekiel's "Jewish Wedding in Bombay". Written in eleven stanzas of uneven length varying from three line stanza to seven line stanza, the poem depicts

Jewish marriage tradition and shows the inherent contradiction in it. The irony in the first stanza is employed through three characters—bridegroom, bride and her mother. The poem begins abruptly with a colloquial tone which is potentially mocking;

> Her mother shed a tear or two but wasn't really/ crying. It was the thing to do, so she did it enjoying every moment. The bride laughed when I/ sympathised, and said don't be silly.

This was followed by the custom like bride's brothers hiding a shoe of the bridegroom and making him pay for getting it back and father-in-law asking the groom how much dowry he expected and finally the ritual of marriage was solemnized.

Thus, says protagonist:

> I remember the breaking of that glass and the congregation/clapping which signified that we were well and truly married/according to Mosaic Law....

There was nothing solemn about it. It is a mechanical observance of rituals devoid of religious seriousness. "Who knows how much belief we had?" asks the poet. This lack of belief makes marriage futile after ten years when a serious quarrel breaks out between the husband and the wife. Ezekiel aptly describes the situation and then gives a twist to the relationship between the couple with a very witty observation. This is how the poem comes to an end:

> More than ten years passed before she told me that/ she remembered being very disappointed. Is that all/ there is to it? She had wondered....
>
> During our first serious marriage quarrel she said why did/ you take away my virginity from me? I would gladly have/ returned it, but not one of the books I had read instructed/ me how. (*Collected Poems 1952-1988*, 130-31)

This kind of witty observation dives deep into human heart and makes us ponder over the question of breaking of family relationship, when the past can't be altered. The question of returning or restoring virginity will remain unanswered for all time to come.

Let me take ecocriticism and apply it to A.K. Ramanujan's "A River". Richard Kerridge in his well-known article, "Environmentalism and Ecocriticism" says,—"Ecocriticism is literary and cultural criticism from an environmentalist view point. Texts are evaluated in terms of their environmentally harmful or helpful effects. Beliefs and ideologies are assessed for their environmental implication" (Waugh 530).

Ramanujan makes a daring effort to penetrate beyond the veil of illusion and unfold the grim truth behind the devastation caused by the river. He does not give a traditional song of praise for the full river; instead, he narrates what he sees as the villagers' 'real experience'. No doubt, the river is beautiful when quiet in the summer, but when it floods it causes suffering that is not at all poetic. The visitor to the village reports what really happens, in the language of a common villager.

Ramanujan resents the lack of imagination on the part of the poets to see into the grim reality. "The poets sang only of the floods" and that is what Ramanujan seems to resent. The rise of water during flood may be exciting but it also causes losses and damages to human life and property. The visitor in the poem rightly reports about water "rising/ on the bathing places, and the way it carried off three village houses". Not only that; what is still more shocking is the loss of cattle and human lives:

> One pregnant woman
> and a couple of cows
> named Gopi and Brinda, as usual.

The phrase 'as usual' is tinged with irony. The callous attitude of the people to look at flood casually has been criticised. Surely, we cannot enjoy flood when it kills human lives. The image of 'pregnant woman' is significant for it involves two generations, the present and the future. The suggestion implicit in the image is that flood not only harms the present generation but also the future. Thus, the destruction caused by flood has deep and far reaching consequences. Unlike Wordsworth, "a Worshipper of Nature" Ramanujan is an observer of Nature, and therefore, he does not turn a blind eye to the devastating aspect of it.

Theory of Diaspora, and Postcolonialism can be applied to Kamala Das's "Home is a Concept", O.P. Bhatnagar's "Look Homeward Angel", and Keki N. Daruwalla's "Migrations". In "Home is a Concept", Kamala Das describes the plight of expatriate, immigrant and diasporic writers for whom the concept of home has become burdensome. An immigrant or diasporic writer may accept another country as his home but does that country accept him as its' own on par with the natives? Some are torn between the country they left behind and the country they adopt as their own. Hence, they are suspended between two words—neither at home, here or there.

> The unwanted wait here, and there for aeroplanes
> clutching at heavy briefcases that hold
> the papers to be read at seminars,
> passports, visas and photographs of laughing
> children. The unwanted carry heavy bags
> and overcoats but the heaviest language
> they tote is pain. If home is a concept
> they shall not know it....
>
> (*Only the Soul Knows How to Sing* 105)

If Kamala Das's "Home is a Concept" explains diasporic situation, O.P. Bhatnagar's "Look Homeward Angel" exposes the intention behind migration and disastrous consequences of migratory movements. The poems opens with a declarative statement:

> I don't blame my friends settled abroad
> Far off in England and Mozambique,
> America, Australia or Madrid,

Bhatnagar compares the migrant Indians to the migratory birds and regrets that unlike the birds, these people never return home. They forget the "country that once brought them up/ splitting water with sun rays" and build "homes away from home". The poet thinks that one of the reasons behind migration is to earn more. So these people fail to "look beyond glamour and gold". Making a reference to history and myth, Bhatnagar says,

> Even Greece had its Ulysses
> Who brought his ships back home

but our Heroes make no myths
And our imagination no Homer
(*An Anthology of Indian English Poetry* 1992: 38)

We can apply myth criticism to some of the poems including Kamala Das's "Radha" and Shiv K. Kumar's "Lord Krishna to Arjuna". Kumar makes use of national myth to explain the doctrine of Karma and how one can be detached in life. Kumar writes:

Look here at those faces of your ancestors,
blurred in the primordial mist. You cannot
recognise any of them, nor do they know
who you are.
O Lord.
Can an act be divorced from the thought
of recompense?
That's man's ultimate frailty, O Warrior,
to know what lies beyond the horizon,
to know the end even before the beginning,
(*Thus Spake the Buddha* 51)

Our poets seem to have paid heed to R. Parthasarathy's exhortation:

How long can foreign poets
Provide the staple of your lines?
Turn inward, scrape the bottom of your past.
(*Rough Passage*)

Gender Studies, Gay and Lesbian criticism can be applied to Kamala Das's "The Looking Glass" and many other poems. Kamala Das, as it were, gives a clarion call to women to surrender to men in love. It is the body that matters. Our fate lies in our body. She writes:

Getting a man to love you is easy...
Gift him all,
Gift him what makes you woman, the scent of
Long hair, the musk of sweat between the breasts,
The warm shock of menstrual blood, and all your
Endless female hungers.
(*The Looking Glass*)

Ezekiel's "Nudes 1978" makes a delightful reading. The poem is in fourteen sections which lays emphasis on the consummation of love. Queer theorists would be delighted to make an explication of it. The poem begins with an assertion on body given to nakedness:

> This body has a name,
> Or the name has a body...
> Sensuality—
> a word that stands by itself, or
> rather, lies down and stretches out
> you touch it, smell it, give yourself
> to every movement...
> Identified obsessive in
> this hunger-making paradise.
>
> (*Collected Poems* 247)

Judith Butler's *Bodies that Matter: On the Discursive Limits of Sex* (1993) is an ideal critical text to analyse the erotic poems of Kamala Das and Nissim Ezekiel.

Apart from the old generation of poets who dominated the poetic scene between 1950s and 1980s, there are a number of poets who appeared between 1990 and 2011. Bibhu Padhi (1951-) is a remarkable poet in the second Generation. His fourth book of verse, *Painting the House* (1999) marks the culmination of his themes and techniques employed in his first three books. He has combined something of Ezekiel and Ramanujan in this book of verse. For instance poems like "House Lizards" and "Portrait of a Family" remind us of Ezekiel's "Night of the Scorpion" and Ramanujan's "Small Scale Reflections of a Great House" in evoking natural scenes in Indian situation. House Lizards are said to be on the side of truth and therefore, believable. This is how Padhi puts it:

> They are believed to be right, always,
> When we differ on a critical point, from behind
> the piles of old newspapers will come the words:
> True, true.

They belong to reptilian group and are taken to be the 'preservers of ancient memories'.

"A Portrait of a Family" reflects on an aged old sick woman, whose husband and child are worried about her inevitable end. The man puts his hand on 'her cheeks, her forehead and lips/ over her fingers that look delicate still' to ascertain whether she is alive. The poem ends with the protagonist's longing for the old woman's long life:

> As I write this, I can almost hear a line
> travel back through the early sun and bird cries:
> You build this home and I only wish
> You had lived a little longer to see
> how, after you, it broke and crumbled—
> inspite of me, inspite of me.

Padhi's poetry is evocative in nature. The language is polished, neat, chiselled. In his use of language Padhi is with Ezekiel, Ramanujan and Parthasarathy. He is successful in acclimatizing an indigenous tradition to English language.

In Shanta Acharya's (1952-) *Not this, Not that* (1994) and *Numbering Our Day's Illusions* (1995), there is a longing for serenity, and calm of mind. She tries to come to terms with herself. Eliot once said, 'People may change and smile but the agony abides.' This seems to be true in case of Shanta Acharya. Memory is a burden that needs to be overcome. Poem after poem she tries to redeem her past and come to terms with reality that baffles her. In "Highgate Cemetery" she says,

> In the unmapped terrain within us we busy
> in terraced catacombs painful memories.
> If only we could let them grow out of us like trees.

She harks on the same theme in another poem called 'Sleep'.

> It is terrible to live with memory
>
> the beginning of all our suffering.

With the advancing years comes the regret for the past and uncertainty for the future. Thus, she writes:

> I travel towards what end I cannot say—along the way, those I meet and those I don't, all that happens and all that I wait for to happen keep defining me in some

> inexplicable way Daily mirror mocks my wrinkles and streaks of grey.
> ("*Shringara*", *Journal of Literature and Aesthetics*. Jan-June 1998:63)

The voice in her poetry is controlled and submerged, looking before and after. Hence, the prayer to understand the meaning of life and bear sufferings with courage and determination.

> ... I have to pray and wait
> for life's meaning to unfold itself to me
> ("The Poet's RSVP")
> Teach me how to find myself in these palaces of art, that
> I may learn to love and suffer with my heart
> ("An Italian Prayer")

Apart from the thematic contents, the language is highly evocative of the scenes depicted in her poetry. The form in her poetry is controlled, and the choice of words and images is appropriate. Acharya has contributed to the creation of an Indian English idiom by using innovative language in her poetry and that is not a mean achievement.

Meena Alexander is one of the well-known Indian English poets of post-1980 Period, who has become an expatriate poet in recent years. Her poetry can be studied profitably along with the poetry of Sujata Bhatt, Rukmani Bhaya Nair and Ranjit Hoskote. She has four collections of poems titled *Stone Roots* (1980), *House of a Thousand Doors* (1985), *River and Bridge* (1995) and *The Shock of Arrival* (1996) to her credit.

A strong political awareness is another striking feature of Alexander's poetry, and this is a trait which few of the contemporary women poets share. In "News of the World", a woman from Cambodia remembers how during the political trouble there, "I/my mother's head in a sack/ ran three days and nights/ through a rice-field." "The Young of Tiananmen" is a moving tribute to martyrs of the notorious Tiananmen Square massacre, "as blood swallowed them whole". "Prison Cell" is an imaginative reconstruction of Nelson Mandela's experience in prison, whether "even an ant, a fly/ would be company".

Sujata Bhatt (1956-), a promising poet has a number of collections of poems to her credit such as *Brunizem* (1988), *Monkey Shadows* (1991), *The Striking Rose* (1995), *Point No Point : Selected Poems* (1997) and *My Mother's Way of Wearing a Sari* (2000). A widely travelled poet, she reflects on her experiences both inside the country and abroad in her poetry.

Nissim Ezekiel and Kamala Das are credited with creating a new idiom in Indian English Poetry by bringing everyday conversational language into the realms of poetry. 'The poetry of popular impersonation' in some of Ezekiel's poetry, endears him to the readers. Poems like, "Healers", "Hangover" "The Patriot", "The Professor", "Ganga", "Entertainment" and "Good bye party for Miss Pushpa T.S." are written in this mode. These poems can be read well by the application of Reader-Response Criticism.

Indian English poetry had its hay day between 1960s and 1980s. Then Indian English fiction came centre stage and became internationally visible thanks to the Man Booker Prize and other Commonwealth Prizes and Pulitzer Prize for a writer of Indian origin like Jhumpa Lahiri. References have already been made to a group of new poets who appeared in the poetic scene between 1990 and 2011. They are C.P. Surendran, Gopi Krishan Kottoor, Makarand Paranjape, Robin S. Ngangom, Ranjit Hoskote, Hoshang Merchant, E.V. Ramakrishnan, Rabi K. Swain, Prabhanjan Mishra, Rukmani Bhaya Nair, Leela Gandhi and a host of others. Some of them are full of promises and potentiality, and one hopes that they would gain academic acceptability and national and international visibility in the years to come. I would like to close this chapter with a quotation for Nissim Ezekiel's "Irani Restaurant Instructions"; which should be the call of the new poets to the readers.

> If not satisfied tell us
> otherwise tell others.

WORKS CITED

Board of Editors. *An Anthology of Indian English Poetry*. Calcutta: Oxford University Press, 1992, Print.

Bloom, Harold. *The Western Canon*. London: McMillan, 1995. Print.

Das, Bijay Kumar. *New Readings in Indian English Literature.* Bareilly: PBD, 2011. Print.

——. *Post Modern Indian English Literature.* New Delhi: Atlantic Publishers, 2010. Print.

Ezekiel, Nissim. *Collected Poems 1952-1988.* Delhi: OUP, 1989. Print.

Kerridge, Richard. "Environmentalism and Ecocriticism". *Literary Theory and Criticism.* Ed. Patrician Waugh. New Delhi: OUP, 2006. Print.

Kumar, Shiv K. *Thus Spake the Buddha.* Delhi: UBSPD, 2002. Print.

Mahapatra, Jayanta. "The Inaudible Resonance in English Poetry in India". *The Literary Criterion*, 15:1, 1980. Print.

——. *Relationship.* Cuttack: Chandrabhaga Society, 1982. Print.

5

Jayanta Mahapatra to Jeet Thayil: The Achievements of Sahitya Akademi Award Winning Indian English Poets

Between 1981 and 2012 over a span of thirty-two years only eight Indian English poets have won the Sahitya Akademi Award. The names include Jayanta Mahapatra, Nissim Ezekiel, Keki N. Daruwalla, Kamala Das, Shiv K. Kumar, Dom Moraes, A.K. Ramanujan and Jeet Thayil in that order. The books of poems which were chosen for the coveted award include *Relationship* (1981), *Latter-Day Psalms* (1983), *The Keeper of the Dead* (1984), *Collected Poems,* Vol. 1 (1985), *Trapfalls in the Sky* (1987), *Serendip* (1994), *The Collected Poems of A.K. Ramanujan* (1999) and *These Errors are Correct* (2012). The purpose of this chapter is to show how far these eight books of poems contribute to the growth and development of Indian English Literature leading to the achievements of these poets. Here, I am reminded of F.O. Mathissen's *The Achievement of T.S. Eliot* which elicited an angry response: "The Achievement"? "What achievement?" from other critics. In the same way, when I say, 'the Achievements of these eight poets', it is bound to evoke a counter response. At the outset, let me say that these poets are achievers and proceed with an evaluation of their poetry in order to establish their position in India and abroad.

Of the eight books of poems chosen for the national award, only *Relationship* is a single long poem in twelve sections. This poem is built on history, myths and architecture of the land of Odisha. It can also be read as a memory poem. The opening lines set the tone of the poem:

> Once again one must sit back and bury the face/ in this earth of forbidding myth...yield to the virtuous water of the hidden springs/ of the Mahanadi,/ the mystery of secret rights that make up destiny. (9)

The texture and structure of the poem are built weaving history, myths, legends of once upon a time heroic state of Odisha, as it used to be called Kalinga in ancient times. This reminds me of Eliot's choice of titles of individual sections of *Four Quartets*: "Burnt Norton", "East Coker", "The Dry Salvages" and "Little Gidding".

Mahapatra has created a poem dovetailing history and geography of Odisha. The Mahanadi, the largest river of Odisha on whose bank is situated Cuttack, the birth place of the poet, Konarka, the pride of Odisha, Lord Jagannath, the sacrifice of heroic Odias who laid down their lives fighting against the cruel Emperor Ashoka who turned to Buddhism after the war, Chilika, the lovely lake of Odisha, Goddess Durga whose image is built of clay every year for worship by the people, the myth of the banished princess of Odia folktale who had been turned into magnolia tree—all these and much more by implication have gone into the texture of the poem, as the poet seeks to build his relationship with the land of his birth. The poem evokes history going back to 261 BC when Emperior Asoka invaded Kalinga and ruthlessly killed thousands of Odias whose blood turned the Daya river red. Not only the poet's maritime ancestors were warriors but they were also traders who used to go to Indonesia, Phillippines for trade and business. New historicists will have a field day in analyzing *Relationship* on the basis of 'textuality of history' and 'historicity of the text'.

Jayanta Mahapatra has given an alternative history of an ancient land of Odisha, which will please the postcolonial critics. This poem was first published in US, and therefore, can be appropriately taken an example of writing back to the centre ("The Empire Writes Back"). Konarka temple is an embodiment of Odishan architecture and a repository of Odishan heritage. The poet's note on the poem, *Relationship* in the manner of Eliot's explanatory notes on *The Waste Land* unfolds the Odishan myth and legend:

> Konarka: The superb 13th century stone temple on the sea, shaped to a monumental chariot and dedicated to the Sun God, is now in a state of ruin. The twenty-four carved wheels with their rich decorations, the seven horses, the magnificent panel of elephants at the base, the figures in the innumerable niches, show the moods and phases of human life compellingly. Its gods and goddesses, *gandharvas* and *apasaras,* the supple women with their entwining serpent bodies, the elaborate latticework—all these represent the Oriya craftsman's search for the beatific vision in the realm of art and aesthetics.... Legend goes that the crowning slab of the temple could only be fitted into place by a 12-year-old boy, the son of the chief architect or the work, after all attempts to do so by the 1200 artisans had failed in 12 long years. Later, the boy jumped to his death from the top of the finished temple to save his father's name and honour in a supreme act of sacrifice (41).

History, myth and legend intertwined in the image of Konarka, keep the memory of the poet alive. In the true Indian tradition memory has played a keyrole in the making of the poem. After Section I, the poet turns to his family history and personalizes his ancestry. References to mother, father and grandfather abound in the poem. The poet probes his origin and traces it back to the shores of Konarka and the clay of Cuttack in his attempt to build relationship with the past. He writes:

> I know I can never come alive
> if I refuse to consecrate at the altar of my origins....
> (Section IV)

He employs the Christian theological word 'consecrate' to explain his birth appropriately and personalize his ancestry. He tells in the opening section of the poem, 'my existence lies in the stones' and asserts it in the following lines:

> Only that the stones were my very own,
> waiting as mother or goddess or witch
> as my birth feeds on them (Section I).

The shadow of Eliot looms large on *Relationship*. We will do well to remember that it is not important what a poet borrows or imitates but what he does with it. Mahapatra has skillfully organized different images to build his relationship with the land of his birth. No wonder, the poet states clearly what he has done in course of the poem: "I tried to speak the myth of sleep and action,/ in the hope of soothing myself and those others,..." and feels emboldened to declare, "Fear of my guilt, I bid you farewell" (Section XII).

If Jayanta Mahapatra lays emphasis on 'history', 'time' and 'myth', Nissim Ezekiel reiterates geography, contemporaneity, and landscape in his poetry. Its an irony of fate that Ezekiel got Sahitya Akademi Award after Mahapatra. *Latter-Day Psalms* (1982) contains "poetry of popular impersonation" (G.S. Fraser's Coinage), a cycle of fourteen poems on love and sex titled *Nudes 1978*, a satirical poem on Jewish Wedding, a minority poem, three postcard poems, two poems from "Songs for Nandu Bhende" and ten poems from *Latter-Day Psalms*. Ezekiel excels in the ironic mode. One important trait of his poetry is conversational language marked by wit. He mocks at the hypocrisy of people who ensnare the credulous fools in the name of faithcure and religious beliefs. In "Healers" he says about the people who come for "buying cures" fall a prey to the healers. These healers pose that they know the way to success.

> The incantations hand
> in the polluted air
> Sex is prohibited or allowed.
> Meat and drink are prohibited
> or allowed.... The Master
> knows the secret....
> It does not matter
> if you teach or advertise.
> God's love remains your heritage.

"Hangover" is a hilarious poem written on the backdrop of Bangala Desh War, the deep meaning of it is highly ironical. The anti-thesis based on binaries mark the trivialities under the grab of seriousness for a cause. This is how the poem goes:

Half the day hazy with the previous night.
The non-drinker drinking, non-smoker smoking....
The foreigners and the foreign returned.
The expensive menu and the shadow of Marx.
The Biryani Hyderabadi and the sighs of Bangala Desh
The sea-through dress and the show-nothing sari.
The fog in the head and the sense of success.
The music Indian and the language English.

Binary oppositions reinforce the meaning which is highly ironical. Ezekiel takes a dig at people who are given to hypocrisy.

Ezekiel's colloquial language, conversational tone marked by wit immediately establishes a rapport with the readers and people. Reader-Response Criticism is the appropriate method of criticism to read and enjoy Ezekiel's poetry. Let us take a well-known poem called, "Jewish Wedding in Bombay" for analysis. The opening stanza immediately establishes a rapport with the readers and sets the tone of the poem. The implicit irony heightens the meaning of the poem. He writes:

Her mother shed a tear or two but wasn't really
crying. It was the thing to do, so she did it,
enjoying every moment. The bride laughed when I
sympathized, and said don't be silly.

After 'breaking the glass' and congregation clapping, the marriage was declared to be solemnized. Then comes the observation:

I don't think there was much
that struck me as a solemn or beautiful.
Mostly we were amused, and so were the others
who knows how much belief we had?

What comes in for criticism in the poem is the rituals we mechanically observe in our country.

The marriage fell into rough weather, when the wife complained after ten years being disappointed in their relationship.

Then came the quarrel of a serious nature, when the wife angrily asked, "Why did you take away virginity from me?" Ezekiel ends the poem with wit in the manner of John Donne:

> I would gladly have
> returned it, but not one of the books
> I had read instructed me how.

Virginity once lost is lost for ever. Like belief either it is there or not there and is not reversible. Ezekiel's wit is imbued with humour. That's is why it is not dry but highly enjoyable. We laugh with the poet but not at him.

Eroticism in Sanskrit literature is depicted freely and frankly. Speaking of love and sex an Indian poet may look upto Sanskrit poets for inspiration. English poetry is no match to ancient Indian literature in matters of depiction of sex and sensuality. That is why Ezekiel turned to Sanskrit poets for inspiration and wrote a cycle of love poems called "Nudes 1978". A cycle of fourteen poems each in fourteen lines without stanza division, "Nudes 1978" begins with the question of identity of name and body 'possessed and possessing'. Deviating from John Donne's Canon of love and identity, "Let's possess one world, each hath one and is one" ("The Good Morrow"), Ezekiel describes love vis-a-vis body, without losing identity.

> We cannot be transcribed: how
> express identity
> in the formal feeling? She and I
> limbs intertwined, retain our names
>
> ("Nudes 1978": I)

"Nudes 1978" is about sex through various persons. The woman teaches the man how to woo and have sex in "Nudes 1978": III.

> 'You have't learnt to kiss', she said,
> 'Open your mouth a little, yes,
> that's the way' . . .
> Did you enjoy it? No? You have
> to love the other person, then you do . . .
> I love
> your body too, though you're hardly
> my cup of tea.

Ezekiel's unrhymed sonnet sequence dealing with love and sexuality revives the sonnet tradition of love and desire. I am inclined to agree with Bruce King when he says,

> The title suggests a series of nude portraits like a painter's work on a theme during a period of time. This is furthered by the distinction between naked and nude, the former usually referring to bareness, being unclothed, whereas nude is more cultured, more a term from the arts. A model, a dancer, an actor may be nude without shocking the cultured whereas a naked person violates most social norms. The naked is scientific, the nude is cultured. We see the world with a naked eye. People are nudists not nakedists. Ezekiel uses this distinction both to examine the social arts that accompany seduction and to draw a parallel between his poems and a painter's series of nude portraits in which formal qualities and matter are of equal interest. Thus the poems shift rapidly between discussion of the women as forms, as arts, as objects of desire, as individuals, and there is a constant secondary significance, as discussion of form and experience can, also refer to the art of poetry (59).

Playing on 'nakedness' and 'nudity', one acceptable and another unacceptable, Ezekiel concludes the poem:

> 'Yes, this is me as I am,'
> naked seen, seeing nakedness,
> named, flawed in detail,
> womanly and vulnerable

Ezekiel is an brilliant observer of life and people. Contemporary reality is best expressed in the direct conversation, and colloquial rhythm. In a poem called "The Professor" Ezekiel writes simple lines:

> These are days of family planning.
> I am not against. We have to change with times.
> Whole world is changing. In India also
> We are keeping up. Our progress is progressing
>
> ("The Professor")

The implicit irony becomes explicit in the last line quoted above, as the poet enforces it with the following two lines:

> Old values are going, new values are coming
> Everything is happening with leaps and bounds.
> ("The Professor")

Ezekiel's poetry communicates before it is understood. That is the hallmark of good poetry if Eliot is to be believed in. Wit, irony, parody, anti-thesis and aboveall humour give a distinct identity to Ezekiel's poetry. Seriousness and levity go together in Ezekiel's poetry. As he describes the contemporary Indian scene, the readers go along with him. To read his poetry is to see an actor enacting the contemporary scene, in which the readers can participate. His poetry bears the indelible mark of Indianness in it. The readers respond to his poetry spontaneously and love him more than any other poet in the postcolonial era.

Keki N. Daruwalla's *The Keeper of the Dead* (1982) contains three sections: (i) "The Keeper of the Dead", (ii) "The Unrest of Desire" and (iii) "In the Shadow of the Imambara". Like W.B. Yeats and Ted Hughes, Daruwalla believes that poetry can issue out of violence and power. Predatory birds like Hawk, Eagle can be subject matter for poetry. William Walsh rightly draws our attention to this aspect of Daruwalla's poetry. Walsh writes:

> Violence, framed and controlled, is the theme of several of Daruwalla's best poems whether it be natural violence or human violence, a river in spate or the shooting of a bird or an appalling presence in life itself (142).

"Hawk", the opening poem of *The Keeper of the Dead* celebrates Hawk's movements in the sky. As a predatory bird he preys on crow, mynah, and pigeon in the evening, besides scanning the other birds. Then comes the metaphor,

> Hawking is turned to a ritual, the predator's
> passion homed to an art. ("Hawk")

This is precisely what Daruwalla does in the poem.

The aggressive hawk is symbolic of brute force, energy and violence, which go together for creation. But the 'tamed one' is worse, as it is caught by men and sometimes loses its sight.

He is momentarily blinded, starved,
till his hood is perforated.
Morsels of vision are fed to his eyes
as he is unblended stich by relentic stich. ("Hawk")

The last quoted line bears the echo of W.B. Yeats.

In "The Revolutionary" the image of hawk is employed to symbolize violence. Daruwalla writes:

What hawk would wheel in
with the message tagged to the claws:
"Let shells rain on the Drought-city,
mobilize despair and turn it to murder.

Daruwalla, like Ezekiel excels in ironic mode. He is critical of rituals performed in the country. In "The King Speaks to the Scribe" he takes a dig at offering ghee to burn altar-fires when we do not have enough fuel for human use. Thus, he says,

I am not here
to appease gods. Even they must be ignored
for a while and their altar-fires turn cold.
Men don't have enough fuel to burn their dead.

Some of his memorable poems include, "Pestilence in Nineteenth-century Calcutta", "Mehar Ali, the Keeper of the Dead", "The Night of the Jackals", "The Persi Hell" and "The Coming of the Sefi". Daruwalla is a poet of Indian landscape and contemporary reality. "To My Daughter Rookzain" is a personal poem with a kind of wish to see the daughter fresh for ever. Here goes the wish:

May you live for ever
in the house of words...
Look fresh, like a rain-washed leaf
with a spray of light on it
and may your breath be spiked
as now, with the tang
of mint and clove and cinnamon
(*The Keeper of the Dead* 50)

Daruwalla believes in creating a new idiom in English. Both in form and content his poetry bears his interior signature and almost a kind of made in India stamp on it.

Kamala Das's Award Winning book of verse *Collected Poems* Volume I has variety of themes—love, death, suicide, nostalgia of the maternal grandmother and her house, and above all, an assertion of feminine voice interrogating the patriarchal society. Some of the well-known poems included here are "In Love", "The Suicide", "Evening at the Old Nalapat House", "A Requiem for my Father", "Blood", "Ghanashyam", "The Dance of the Eunuchs" and "Composition". Kamala Das, like Jayanta Mahapatra wants to connect with the past and build relationship. Hence, she personalizes her ancestry. Her poetry is part autobiographical and part confessional. Most of her erotic love poems are written in the confessional mode. The need for love, the 'unending lust' remind her of the pleasure of the body and make her restless in "In Love".

> ...while I walk
> The verandah sleepless, a
> Million questions awake in
> Me, and all about him, and
> This skin-communicated
> Thing that I dare not yet in
> His presence call our love
>
> ("In Love")

She, like John Donne lays emphasis on the consummation of love. Body can't be dispensed with giving priority only to the soul. Here comes the assertion:

> Bereft of soul
> My body shall be bare.
> Bereft of body
> My soul shall be bare.
>
> ("The Suicide")

She mocks at the patriarchal tradition which expects the woman to be an obedient wife. Thus, she says,

> I must pose.
>
> I must pretend,
> I must act the role
> Of happy woman,
> Happy wife.
>
> ("The Suicide")

Love becomes lust when a man forces himself on a woman. In the confessional mode Kamala Das writes:

It required drinks
To hold him down.
To make him love.
But, when he did love,
Believe me,
All I could do was sob like a fool ("The Suicide")

Therefore, the body can't sing in such a situation and it is left to the soul to do so. Thus, comes the bathos:

Only the soul knows how to sing
At the vortex of the sea
("The Suicide")

Its ironical that her next volume of poems is titled, *Only the Soul Knows How to Sing* (1996).

As the poet grows in years, she gathers experience and replaces 'love with guilt'. Realisation is drawn upon her to assert that 'both love and hate are involvements'. Now she comes to the conclusion that 'friendship cannot endure' and 'blood-ties do not satisfy'. Hence, the declaration:

I must let my mind striptease
I must extrude
autobiography
("Composition")

Now the woman of flesh and blood who once pleaded for all kinds of love (hetero as well as lesbian) turns to Lord Krishna and surrenders:

Shyam O Ghanashyam
you have like a fisherman cast your net in the narrows of my mind
And towards you my thoughts today
Must race like enchanted fish....
("Ghanashyam")

The ending of poem with three dots (...) suggests that the poem is not complete but abandoned. This is in keeping with Paul Valery's theory that a poem is never complete but abandoned.

Shiv K. Kumar's *Trapfalls in the Sky* (1986) contains three sections: "On Native Grounds", "Under Alien Skies" and "Genesis". Kumar like metaphysicals puts all his learning into his poetry. Intertextuality is the hallmark of his poetry. His poetry is learned and imagery is complex. Each poem speaks for itself. The title of the book *Trapfalls in the Sky* bears testimony to it.

National identity and Indian landscape go together in Kumar's poetry. "Dal Lake: Srinagar", "Cleansing Ganga", "O Delhi!", "Sunset Over Shimla Hills", and "A Wayside Shiva Temple" are some of his well-known poems on Indian landscape. Like Ezekiel, Kumar also takes a dig at mechanical performance of rituals. The sacred Ganga gets polluted with offering made by the pilgrims to the dead. Thus, Kumar writes:

> It's only when they are carried down the river of time/ that iron sinks into their souls./ The waters then get sullied by ritual and dogma-/ ashes and bones, wilted floral offerings to the dead,/ and the noontime sweat oozing from the saffron—/ striped foreheads of the crocodiles/ whose yawning jaws chant mantras in some obsolete/ tongue. ("Cleansing Ganga", *Trapfalls in the Sky* 35)

Kumar like metaphysical poets brings all his learnings of English literature into his poetry. Irony becomes a tool in Kumar's hand as he takes a dig at long delay in Court judgements. In "Tis Hazari Courts, Delhi" he says,

> There's the Kaurava-Pandava land-wrangle
> still being argued in some haunted chamber—
> the judge snoozy, the lawyers jaded.
> Only the clerk and the crier are wide-awake—
> their palms unclawed like the Pandas'
> at a shrine, controlling all entry
> through the strait gate
> to silence.
> It's the long wait that kills
> the lover, the cancer-patient
> and the petitioner.
>
> (*Trapfalls in the Sky* 23)

The above quoted three lines are modelled on Shakespeare's "Poet, Lover and Lunatic are of Imagination all Compact" and Ezekiel's, "Poet, Lover and Bird Watcher gain by waiting". "Eunuchs" is a highly ironical poem. If in our society the eunuchs are welcome on wedding anniversary, a son's thread ceremony and what Kumar says 'even a cow's first delivery' for they are thought to bring luck for the family, when they themselves have no luck. Hence, the ironical ending:

Between their cymbal-palms, the stray winds
break into song
that bring you blessings from their gods
who themselves died boonless.

(*Trapfalls in the Sky* 42)

The second section of the poem, *Under Alien Skies* contains seven poems written in USA. This section testifies that Indian poets not only write on or about India but they also write about the west. Kumar comes down heavily on fake godmen who continue to trap the innocent people into false belief. Thus, in "Sunday Preacher on TV" he writes:

In the beginning was the word
—not mouthfuls of this godman
Slick as an egg-shell, glib as a macaw.

Kumar like Daruwalla is an imagist poet, "Shakespeare Seminar: Fall 1981", "A Young Female Jogger" are examples of Kumar's apt imagery. He debunks a Professor who has an eye on a lady student. Thus, he says,

Lie with her! Lie on her!
Noses, ears and lips! . . .
Have I like Tiresias, unhooked the mating pair?
....
But the eye, Sheila has no age
no discretion
for even the wrinkled hands are smoothed
by a rabbit's caress. So here I am watching
that silver pendent swing in the vale
of your sophomore breasts.

(Shakespeare Seminar: Fall 1981)

The last section "Genesis" contains six poems on Adam, Eve and the Serpent. This is a unique section that dives deep into the origin of mankind. No Indian English poet has worked on this theme before Kumar. These are remarkable poems on temptation, sin and disinheritance. "Adam to Eve" speaks of Adam's agony and also resolution to go with Eve. Thus, says Adam,

> Forged out of dust, doomed to encounter
> contraries, now I know that to multiply
> is to seek confluence with another tributary,
> that to replenish the earth is to first ravage it
> that to have dominion over my woman
> during day, I must give in after dusk
> that a curse may turn into a boon
> denial into affirmation.
> that every creature that moves
> has a still axis, that no herb
> will ever heal our new wound
> that sings as it bleeds.
> And if to know is to die,
> why not perish together?
>
> (*Trapfalls in the Sky* 74-75)

After the fall, what remains? The desire for redemption. That is what mankind is seeking from the day of their first parents' fall.

Kumar's poetry is marked by wit, humour and irony. It makes us aware of ourselves in our situation. It speaks to us and moves us, we laugh with him but not at him. In the last analysis it delights us.

Serendip (1990) derives its title from "Serendip" the ancient name of Ceylon, presently known as Sri Lanka. It consists of four sections: I "Serendip", II "Steles", III "Barrows" and IV "Other Poems". In an "Introduction" to the book, Moraes states:

> The title sequence of this book is called "Serendip". Ceylon was at one time known to travelers by this name. The associations it has acquired are such that "Serendip" now seems a mythical place. As a child I lived for two years in Ceylon, and in its forests encountered the Veddahs, shy tribesmen who are said to have been the

first inhabitants of the island. My recollections of these people, and of pilgrims with lamps climbing Adam's Peak, are very clear, and in these sonnets I have tried to turn them into myth and symbol. The sequence is a chronological account of actual events in Sri Lanka, but it could be said to have been written in the form of a myth. (10)

The title poem consists of eight sonnets, Prologue and Epilogue—all in sonnet form without formal stanza divisions. It begins with 'the first man's footstep' on 'a hill top' and ends with ethnic war between the Sinhala and the Tamils. The movement of the poem is swift as the poet wants to historicize the text by creating new myths. Needless to say that the dead king, the first man retain 'a relevance'. The landscape of Sri Lanka comes alive in the poem as 'the silent/ Island awaits visitors. The early settlers came by ships and in the words of the poet, 'The settled, they bred'. They gave the Island 'a local habitation and a name'.

They composed a culture:
Symbols scratched on stone
Hewn to build temples.
Thing, Place, Creature,
Named, therefore known

(*Serendip* III)

In the south, the Sinhala and in the north "The Descendants of Elara" raged for a combat as the country prepared for a parliamentary form of government. Thus, says the poet,

Parliament for an island
Bewildered with new flags.
Old grudges, latent for years
Were nudged, to hate in the north

(*Serendip* VII)

In "Epilogue" speaks of pilgrims 'with lamps resume/from Memory' and hope to return to 'the summit of the peak'. This poem is built on history and turn to contemporary reality making an amalgam of history, memory, myth and geography. As the poet rightly says,

> ... I am fascinated by history, and to me the entire human past has the quality of myth, and myths as such are intertwined with all history, and with all the past. My imaginative processes operate like this, and I cannot change them. It is possible to create a realistic myth, and to populate a myth with one's own realities and one's own experience. (10)

There are three ways in which a poet makes use of myths: One, by evoking archetypal myths for the benefit of mankind, two, by employing national myths (as Moraes has done here) for eliciting the participation of the people of the nation and finally by creating personal myths. Sri Lankan history and myths are reinforced in *Serendip* to historicize the past and write the nation.

The second section "Steles" contains ten poems in quatrain form which contrasts with "Serendip". Bruce King makes an apt observation on "Steles" in the following words:

> While the "Steles" (inscribed upright pillars) sequence is more hermetical than 'Serendip' there are numerous organizing themes and motifs. One strand contrasts the permanence of writing with the impermanence of action, and shows that greatness needs the monuments of art to be remembered. Another strand is about Moraes, or the writer. This theme is clear from the first with its version of Genesis. 'The word works. The world doesn't.' The sequence appears to be almost simultaneously in an ancient past and in the present. 'At my orders great armies/ Shuffled in step to conquer.' 'What is this airdrift from Chile/ And murdered Allende, to freeze me?' History, contemporary politics, the role of art, eroticism, the apocalyptic, and the personal exist side by side. (176)

The poet knows that it is the word that works but not the world. Word outlines the world. Hence, the Steles. The appeal is, "put one word on my stele". Then comes the contrast;

> The word walks to the finger
> On the key of the machine
> The world rocks on its axis,
> Like a sleepy sentry. (Steles V)

The shadow of T.S. Eliot looms large. In *Four Quartets* Eliot dwells on the movement of words and with consummate skills:

> Words move, music move
> Only in time, but that which is only living
> can only die ("Burnt Norton").

Dom Moraes is in line with Eliot. The 'word' for Moraes 'works', 'moves' and 'dances'. 'The words are firmly placed' and they build in the world ("The worlds and words build and build"). Then comes the personal sorrow for the dead wife. The past comes alive as the poet becomes nostalgic of the years gone by.

> She in her youth arose
> Shape moulded by mild winds
> Hips to launch many ships
> Nippled bowels of cream and honey. (VII)

'Time' is personified and polished. The image of Stele is employed to drive home the concept of passing time. Moraes writes:

> On my stele, mark colours
> Appraisals of south and wind
> The scented flesh of my wife
> A Siamese cat, dachshund
> And me, unsteady of mind (VI)

Time is like a flowing river which flows at its own will.

> Time and the river aflame
> with the explosion of suns (VIII)

Then comes the realization, that every body has to go one day. Hence, a place is needed on stele. The poet asks:

> What was I will not be
> After this day's dying.
> Paint on my stele
> Bones and a lark flying (IX)

Of all the Award winning poets, Moraes is the only one who was interested in 'archaeological excavations' and like Eliot, he was absorbed in anthropology. And again like W.B. Yeats writing "Sailing to Byzantium" after seeing the Byzantine art gallery, Moraes writes two cycles of poems "Steles" and "Barrows" after visiting museums in foreign countries. He makes this clear in the following words:

> The behaviour of people, even those in myths, has possessed certain common denominators and factors for thousands of years. The dead, inclusive of the recent dead, seem to me to be absorbed into myth by their dying. I do not mean to sound Delphic about this, only to say that it is what happens in my mind, and what I have tried to convey in the two cycles of poems called "Steles" and "Barrows". I have spent a good deal of time at archaeological sites and in museums, in Greece and Sweden. This was not so much to collect information on tombs and the relics they contain as to "get the feel" of these places, for my own pleasure. (10-11)

What is important is to find a pattern in history and myth in order to recreate the past in contemporary terms. In a cycle of ten poems containing five quatrains each the poet enters into dialogue with the dead in barrows. In "Barrows" Section III and IV the dead tempts the living with gold and ornaments. Moraes makes it explicit:

> I hear you tap at my tomb.
> Ornaments and cloth are with me...
> lunch with me in my stone womb.
> I'll give you hieroglyphs and swords
> (Section III)

A dead woman in the grave laments the loss of gifts brought by her husband for her, as she died of "the flux and fever" before using 'any of his gifts'. The irony is that he 'buried them all with me'. In another poem (Section VII) a woman implores upon her husband to come back for the sake of their daughter. The woman from the barrow says,

> The child died in my belly
> while you were still in Africa
> one of your business trips
> over a long winter.
> I died too....
> They preserved with chemicals

Here in the Nordic Museum.
Our daughter waits to see you,
Comeback soon from Africa.
(Section VII)

Bruce King makes a valid observation on this poem in the following words:

> "Barrows" is another sequence of poems, here of ten monologues in different personae, each in five quatrains. The poems celebrate the Viking culture of Scandinavia, its vigour, daring, brutality, and conquests while recognizing that it now exists only in monuments. Such warrior achievement is precarious in contrast to how art memorializes, although necessarily falsifying. (178)

Bruce King also comments on the final section of "Barrows":

> In the final monologue a long dead Swedish guard recalls being killed by the Danes, 'Berserkers with honed helmets./ Bellaxes, torches flaming.' Burnt alive within a watchtower his death is marked by a runestone. What the modern tourists read has become his identity. 'Telling me who I am'. Writing and other arts tell us who are and will be our histories. (178)

Memory of the past and devastations caused by death unnerve the poet. He writes:

Words like snails on the paper,
You intend not to write
Your typewriter's tired,
Thinking too much of death.
("Intentions")

Moraes notes make the poems easily accessible to the readers. He writes:

> The "Other Poems" which form the last section of the book were written after the sequence "Serendip", and the two cycles. Not all these pieces use myth as a technical device, but some do. In "New Year", for example, the ancient practice of human sacrifice at specified times of year is the centre of the poem. In "Spring Song", the

> figures of Dracula, a modern myth is used in the context of an Indian city. I do not think there is any more I can usefully say. To try and take oneself seriously is to set oneself up for the target practice of critics.... (11)

Landscape of the place and the practice of the people in Ceylon (Sri Lanka) go hand in hand in Moraes's poetry. History and time are two major determiners of his poetry. From impersonality theory of poetry there is a turn away to personal things. No wonder, the poem closes with a personal poem on the death of his wife Leela-Claire.

A.K. Ramanujan is the only Indian English poet to win the Sahitya Akademi Award posthumously in 1999, for *The Collected Poems of A.K. Ramanujan.* It contains four books of poems, *The Striders* (1966), *Relations* (1971), *Second Sight* (1986) and *The Black Hen* (1995). He has a variety of themes, and competence of execution of them in suitable imagery. He is an imagist poet in the manner of T.S. Eliot and Ezra Pound. History, myth, folk tales and contemporary Indian scene are his favourite themes.

His well-known poems include "Small-Scale Reflections on a Great House", "Compositions of Despair", "A River" (much anthologized poem), "Prayers to Lord Murugan", "Obituary", "The Guru", "No Fifth Man" and "Death and the Good Citizen". A keen observer of life and people, Ramanujan brings out the importance of joint family life in "Small-Scale Reflections on a Great House". But he is also equally keen to show the funny aspects of it. He writes:

> Things come in every day...
> behind windows with holes in them.

The cyclic process of life is depicted in "Birthdays". The four elements of life earth, air, water and fire recur in the ever cyclic order of life and death. These four elements which sustain the life, also consume it. Birth days are observed for institutions as well as persons. As Ramanujan puts its:

> Even universities,
> art museums, apple trees
> that recycle the seasons,
> and inventions like guns

have their birthdays
like St Francis, Shakespeare,
Gandhi and Washington
marked on calendars.
("Birthdays")

"The Guru" like Ezekiel's "Guru" is a satire on the so-called Gurus. The Guru's bias against women was not shared by the disciple. The disciple defied him.

I gave the dog his bone, the parrot
His seed, the pet snake his mouse
Forgave the weasel his tooth
Forgave the tiger his claw,
And left the guru to clean his own shoe
For I remembered I was a man born of woman.
("The Guru")

Ramanujan writes with Tamil-Kannada tradition in his bones. His poetry is a veritable apotheosis of the tradition and the Individual talent. His thematic range and technical virtuosity endears him to readers both at home and abroad.

Jeet Thayil is with Dom Moraes in giving notes to his book of poems, *These Errors are Correct.* Thayil's poetry is full of intertextuality. The ground swell of suffering caused by the death of his wife at a tender age forms the bedrock of Thayil's book of verse. The loss is enormous. No wonder the book begins with irreparable loss.

I lost the house. I lost the way home....
My wife died.
("Not Remembering" 1)

References to Jesus, Buddha and even to Gandhi is an attempt to Philosophize the personal sufferings in life.

It wan n't that people
wanted a new life, they didn't
want the old one....
Gandhi said Beethoven said Buddha said
("Not Remembering" 3)

All these three—Gandhi, Beethoven and Buddha could not heal the wound. Hence, the refrain

> My wife died. I
> want to build a cathedral where birds
> can worship.
>
> ("Not Remembering" 5)

"Premonition" is a sequence of ten poems written for the wife and are dedicated to her. This is like Dom Moraes's poem, "Future Plans" written for his dead wife. Thayil's memory of his dead wife lingers, 'Sunday speaks, but only about you'. Forgetting is not easy. Thus, he says,

> Everybody forgets every dear thing
> I know how it goes. This is safe keeping. (" Premonition" 9)

The last poem in the Sequence is an astonishingly compact and memorable poem. The separation is irrevocable. The agony abides.

> When it rains, the dead descend, you appear,
> the smell of rainwater in your hair,
> wearing the ring I placed on your finger,...
> your lips, clear of the color you wear,
> are not new to me, are lovely and bare,
>
> ("Premonition" 10)

The lovers' perennial question, "Will you forget me if I die?" is disturbing. The wound is never healed. 'If I forget you, let everything die,' asserts the lover again and again. Then come the hour of final separation.

> When it rains the dead ascend, disappear
> where we cannot follow, into the living air.
>
> ("Premonition" 10)

The last but one linc, "When it rains, the dead ascend, disappear" should have been, "when it stops, the dead ascend, disappear". That would be more appropriate as binary opposition to the first line of the poem. This sonnet in the form of two line and four line stanzas alternates giving vent to the feeling of loss on the death of his wife, Shakti Bhatt, in which the book, *These Errors are Correct* is foregrounded. No wonder, it appears on the jacket of the book.

Two poems, "The Sonneteer" and "After Brodsky" are intertextual poems making references to the life of Dom Moraes and the poem of Joseph Brodsky called "For E.R." ("A Second Christmas by the Shore"), Memory, nostalgia and brooding for lost love are some of the key themes in Jeet Thayil's poetry. "Nativism", "Superpower" and "The New Island" are some of Thayil's successful poems. "Movement is bliss" for Thayil and therefore he changes places from poem to poem. But eventually he comes back from where he started. "The end is where we start from", Eliot's words in *Four Quartets* seem to have influenced Thayil most. "I am back where my life and I parted ways" ("The Penitent") bears echoes of Eliot.

Lost love continues *to* haunt him poem after poem. "I make my home with you, in transit" ("Flight"). The realization is finally dawns on the poet who says, "Misfortune works in cycles beyond time" (2007). With this Thayil gains an insight into life. The poems ends appropriately with the following words:

> I'm walking with you, hand in hand,
> hoping you remember, this is my name,
> here's where we met, this is the time
> we had together, an hour and a day.
>
> ("2007")

In conclusion let us assess what are the achievements of these eight Sahitya Akademi Award Winning poets. One, Indian English poetry has turned global at their hands as they expanded the thematic range of it by including the landscape and people of other countries. Two, these poets have given a new idiom called Indian English to English language. As a result, Indian poetry is distinguished from African poetry, Australian poetry, Caribbean poetry, Canadian poetry and Newzealand poetry—all written in English language. Three, Indian English poetry is the only Pan Indian poetry written in the last half of the twentieth century and early twenty-first century. Regional poetry or Bhasha poetry is also Indian poetry but not Pan Indian poetry, as their locale is not the whole country. Last but not the least, Indian English poetry has successfully written back to the west by evoking alternative indigenous history and contemporary landscape and people of the country. Above all, Indian English poetry has turned global in the hands of the leading Indian English poets of the last fifty years.

WORKS CITED

Das, Kamala. *Collected Poems.* Vol. 1, Trivandrum: Self-Published, 1984. Print.

Daruwalla, Keki N. *The Keeper of the Dead.* Delhi: Oxford University Press, 1982. Print.

Ezekiel, Nissim. *Latter-Day Psalms.* Delhi: Oxford University Press, 1982. Print.

King, Bruce. *Three Indian Poets.* New Delhi: OUP, 2005. Print.

Kumar, Shiv K. *Trapfalls in the Sky.* Madras: MacMillan, 1986. Print.

Mahapatra, Jayanta. *Relationship.* New York: The Greenfield Review Press, 1980. rpt. Cuttack: The Chandrabhaga Society, 1982. Print.

Moraes, Dom. *Serendip.* New Delhi: Viking, 1990. Print.

Ramanujan, A.K. *The Collected Poems of A.K. Ramanujan.* Delhi: Oxford University Press, 1995. Print.

Thayil, Jeet. *These Errors are Correct.* Chennai: West Landbooks Pvt. Ltd., 2008. Print.

Walsh, William. *Indian Literature in English.* London: Longman, 1990. Print.

6

Contextualizing the Mythic 'Crow' and 'Fox' in Ted Hughes's Poetry*

In the first two decades of the second-half of the twentieth century (i.e., in the 1950s and 1960s) there was no towering poet to match the talent and calibre of a W.B. Yeats or a T.S. Eliot. Hence, Robert Conquest brought together nine 'Movement Poets'—Philip Larkin, John Wain, Kingsley Amis, Thom Gunn, Elizabeth Jennings, D.J. Enright, John Holloway, Donald Davie and Robert Conquest—in an anthology called *New Lines* in 1956 (Williams 135). When A. Alvarez criticized this anthology as 'academic-administrative verse' in his anthology *The New Poetry* (1962), Robert Conquest answered him in his introduction to *New Lines*-2 (1963) (Rosenthal 200-01) and it is in this volume that he included Ted Hughes. Hughes published his first book of verse, *Hawk in the Rain* in 1957. He acknowledged his indebtedness to poets like Shakespeare, Blake, Yeats and Eliot, who influenced him and inspired his poetic sensibility.

Both Yeats and Eliot made use of national and archetypal myths, and they also created personal myths. Ted Hughes learnt

* This paper is the revised version of the lecture delivered at the National Seminar on "Contextualizing the British Canon: A Reading of the Twentieth-Century Canonical Authors" on 20 February, 2009 organized by the Department of English, Burdwan University, Burdwan.

from them how to make use of myths and to create new myths. It may be mentioned here that there are three ways in which a writer can make use of myths—one, he can make use of national myths, such as 'Trishankhu' in Indian context to show how a person is suspended between two worlds and belongs to both and neither (this is the way we describe the current diasporic persons), two, he can make use of archetypal myths (such as creation myth) which are universal, and three, he can create personal myths as Yeats did in his 'The Second Coming' and prose work "A Vision". Ted Hughes made use of archetypal myths and he also created personal myths. The purpose of this chapter is to re-situate the 'crow' and the 'fox' in the context of myths in Hughes's poetry.

Hughes published his *Crow* volume in 1970 with 59 poems which was enlarged in 1972 with the addition of 7 more poems. Hughes learnt about myth from Robert Graves's *The White Goddess,* Mircea Eliade's *Shamanism* and Paul Radin's *The Trickster.* Rand Brandes makes an interesting observation on Hughes's use of myth in the following words:

> Moving beyond these secondary sources, Hughes immersed himself in the primary works of traditional cultures from the Balkans to Bali. His work as a reviewer of books of and on the 'literature' of traditional peoples and his role as an editor of *Modern Poetry in Translation* (in the mid-1960s), provided a more global mythic framework. Hughes was going door-to-door in the Global village, long before many people knew it existed. Unlike the High Moderns who 'applied' myth to their poetry, Hughes internalized not only the materials of myth, but also its essential elements—its language, rhythms and structures. *Crow* does not 'use' myth, it is myth. Hughes was mythically multi-cultural before the concept was coined. From this perspective crow—as culturally other—may be seen as an early post-colonial response to the new world order.
>
> Hughes's use of Irish myth in *Crow* is one important instance of his cultural diversity.... Crow is related to the Celtic goddess of war and destruction Morrigna,

> a triadic composite that includes Macha, the crow, Morrigan, battle-goddess, and Badbh, referred to as 'Badbh Catha'—the battle crow. (Roberts 515)

Let us take the following extracts from Ted Hughes and from the critics to find out the significance of the mythic crow:

> The first idea of *Crow* was really an idea of a style. In folktales the prince going on the adventure comes to the stable full of beautiful horses and he needs a horse for the next stage and the King's daughter advises him to take none of the beautiful horses that he'll be offered but to choose the dirty, scabby little foal. You see, I throw out the eagles and choose the Crow. (qtd. in Dyson 106)
>
> After having created the world God has a nightmare in the form of a Voice and a Hand which ridicules the creation and particularly God's masterpiece, Man. God claims that his creation has been a complete success and a debate ensues which is interrupted by a message from the world that Man wants God to take life back. God challenges the Nightmare to do better and the Nightmare's response is to create Crow. (qtd. in Gifford and Roberts 116)

Jarold Ramsey explains the importance of crow in the following words:

> In exploring his roots in world folklore, I want to insist that first and last, Crow is Ted Hughes' own astonishing invention, for his own purposes: one might say, admiringly, that he is an addition to folk-literature, not merely something borrowed from it. (qtd. in Sagar 173)

Having said so, let me explore a few poems such as "A Childish Prank", "Crow's First Lesson", "Two Legends" and "Little Blood". Some of these poems have implicit references to Christianity. In "A Childish Prank", Hughes speaks of man's and woman's bodies lying 'without souls' 'on the flowers of Eden'. Crow played mischief and 'bit the worm', God's only son, 'Into two writhing halves'. He gave half to man and the other half to woman. Thus,

Man awoke being dragged across the grass.
Woman awoke to see him coming.
Neither knew what happened.

This marks the beginning of sexuality. As 'God went on sleeping/ Crow went on laughing'.

In "Crow's First Lesson" Hughes gives another instance of the beginning of sexuality:

"A final try," said God. "Now, LOVE."
Crow convulsed, gaped, retched and
Man's bodiless prodigious head
Bulbed out onto the earth, with swivelling eyes,
Jabbering protest—

And Crow retched again, before God could stop him.
And woman's vulva dropped over man's neck and tightened.
The two struggled together on the grass.
God struggled to part them, cursed, wept—

Crow flew guiltily off.

The black colour of 'Crow' reminds us of the primodial dark, that was there in the earth before the light came into existence. Crow symbolizes both space and time, the beginning and the movement. It is both evil and good. It is dark and destructive on the one hand, and life force on the other. The last poem of *The Crow* volume "Littie Blood" is seen as a 'light of hope'. The closing line, 'sit on my finger, sing in my ear, O little blood', is significant. Seamus Heaney, the Irish Nobel Laureate praises this poem by saying, 'I have always tended to read "little blood" as an instance of that kind of transition (from the tragic to the transcendent). It is as if, at the last moment, grace has entered into the crow-cursed Universe' (qtd. in Brandes in, Roberts 517).

In a significant poem called 'Crow and the Birds', Hughes, points out what different birds mean to him. 'When the eagle soared clear through a dawn distilling of emerald', 'the swallow swooped through a woman's song in a cavern', 'the owl sailed clear of tomorrow's conscience', 'the sparrow preened himself of yesterday's promise', 'the goldfinch bulbed in the sun', 'the wryneck crooked in the moon', then as a contrast the 'Crow spraddled head-down in the beach-garbage, guzzling a dropped ice-cream'. No doubt that the crow is dark and ugly and his song is bereft of music. The crow symbolizes the dark aspect of life. But one has to move through the dark to come to light. It is in this sense that the crow can be taken as a gateway to enlightenment.

It is in this context that Edward Larrissy has made an apt observation on *crow*:

> *Crow* can be seen as a descent into hell, or, in alchemical parlance, Melancholy, which is a necessary prelude to resurrection, or the finding of the philosopher's stone. Hughes, with his interest in Jung and alchemy, must have been pleased to reflect that the 'melancholy' or black phase of the alchemical amalgam was known as the 'head of the raven'. I should add that he may have come across a reference specifically to a crow as symbol of the dark stage in Jung's *Alchemical Studies*:
>
> My soul and spirit fast are sinking
> And leave a poison, black and stinking.
> To a black crow am I akin,
> Such be the wages of all sin.
>
> In *Gaudete* Hughes feels he has found the philosopher's stone of spiritual renewal, as the title implies. The right relationship with the feminine, so necessary for this, can be discerned in the symbol of the alchemical union of opposites necessary for the Great Work. The opposites are, chemically, Sulphur and Mercury. But the symbols for them are legion: Fire and Water, Eagle and Serpent, Sun and Moon, King and Queen, Bride and Groom. The union of these opposites, necessary to create the philosopher's stone, is called, in alchemical parlance, a 'Marriage', as in Blake's *The Marriage of Heaven and Hell,* a work which draws on the alchemical tradition. Hirschberg is right to see in the poem 'Bride and groom lie hidden for three days', from *Cave Birds,* an allusion to the alchemical marriage. It is significant that this celebratory poem, in which male and female 'bring each

other to perfection', is so near the sequence's conclusion, marked by a poem called 'The risen'. The soul has to go through the black or melancholy stage, and through a union of opposites, in order to be reborn. A clear allusion to the black part of this process can be seen in a poem near the end of *Adam and the Sacred Nine*:

"The Crow came to Adam"
Who has understood the Crow's love-whisper?
Or the Crow's news?
Adam woke.
The stage of the Crow is necessary to enlightenment. (131-32)

Giving a radio talk for schools on writing in general and his own writing in particular in the early sixties, Hughes called it "Capturing Animals". There is a vital relationship between Hughes' interest in collecting animals and writing poetry. Martin Dodsworth states this aspect of Hughes's poems in the following words:

> The special kind of excitement, the slightly mesmerized and quite involuntary concentration with which you make out the stirrings of a new poem in your mind, then the outline, the mass and colour and clean final form of it in the midst of the general lifelessness, all that is too familiar to mistake. This is hunting and the poem is a new species of creature a new specimen of the life outside your own. (Ford 281)

He turns to the world of animals for two reasons—one, as Hughes notes that 'they have a certain wisdom. They know something special...something perhaps which we are curious to learn' (*The Poetry in the Making* 16). It is through them Hughes 'sees into the life of things' in the same way Wordsworth 'sees into the life of things' through nature. Margaret Dickie Uroff underlines this aspect of Hughes' poetry in the following words:

> Hughes's animals may inhabit the world beyond the human, but as they come into his poems they are creatures made of words, carrying the burden of Hughes vision, and what he sees in them is what he sees to his own

> deepest nature. Animals talk and think and dream only in poems, and when they do so, they express their own world only as it is refracted through the human eyes of the poet. (13)

Secondly, Hughes thinks that "any form of violence—any form of vehement activity invokes the bigger energy, the elemental power circuit of the Universe. Once the contact has been made—it becomes difficult to control. Something from beyond ordinary human activity enters" (Dyson 103).

The two animals which dominate the poetic world of Hughes are the fox and the jaguar. About the fox Hughes writes:

> An Animal I never succeeded in keeping alive is the fox. I was always frustrated: twice by a farmer, who killed cubs I had caught before I could get to them, and once by a poultry keeper who freed my cub while his dog waited. Years after those events I was sitting up late one snowy night in dreary lodgings in London. I had written nothing for a year or so but that night I got the idea I might write something and I wrote in a few minutes the...poem: the first "animal" poem I ever wrote. (qtd. in Usha, V.T. 121)

The 'Fox' is not an ordinary fox. Using the deconstructive terminology we should say that half of the sign of 'fox' is adequate and the other half is to be comprehended by 'trace' for it means something else (may be the creative spirit of man). Hughes, further clarifies:

> It is about a fox, obviously enough, but a fox that is both a fox and not a fox. What sort of a fox is it that can step right into my head where presumably it still sits... smiling to itself when the dogs bark. It is both a fox and a spirit. It is a real fox.... As it is, every time I read the poem the fox comes up again out of the darkness and steps into my head. And I suppose that long after I am gone, as long as a copy of the poems exists, every time anyone reads it the fox will get up somewhere out in the darkness and come walking towards them.
>
> So, you see, in some ways my fox is better than an ordinary fox. It will live for ever, it will never suffer from

> hunger or hounds. I have it with me wherever I go. (*The Poetry in the Making* 20-21)

A much anthologized poem. "Thought Fox" is a thought provoking poem. The deep meaning of the poem cancels out the surface meaning. The poet sitting at night and looking through the window at the sky imagines a fox entering into the loneliness. First comes the nose, then the eyes (i.e., the smell followed by the sight) and then the body, the imagination turns into reality. Then comes the fox.

> It enters the dark hole of the head
> The window is starless still, the clock ticks
> The page is printed.

The fox is symbolic of the creative force that generates poetry. Imagining the fox in the dark is to wait anxiously in loneliness for the poem to be born. Thought—fox is a creative force—a regenerative faculty that results in poetic creation.

E.M.W. Tillyard speaks of two kinds of poetry—'direct' and 'oblique' (qtd. in Kar 35). In direct poetry the surface meaning is the same as the deep meaning. But in oblique poetry one thing is stated in terms of another—the deep meaning is not the same as the surface meaning. Hughes's Crow poems and poems on Fox belong to the second category—i.e., they are oblique poems.

Hughes's Crow Poems, though based on archetypal myths, are in a way Hughes's own creation. They are interpreted best in terms of Hughes's concept of creation, good, and evil. Fox is not portrayed as a cunning animal but as an elusive creative force that needs concentration and loneliness for creative expression. It is Hughes's own creation—a personal myth on the art of writing poetry. His poems on crow and fox have much to offer by way of insight into human nature and creativity. In *Western Canon* Harold Bloom states that "One mark of an originality that can win canonical status for a literary work is a strangeness that we either never altogether assimilate, or that becomes, such a given that we are blinded to its idiosyncrasies," (4). Ted Hughes has amply demonstrated in his poetry these two qualities on the basis of which his claim to canonical status can never be denied.

WORKS CITED

Bloom, Harold. *The Western Canon.* London: Papermac, 1995. Print.

Brandes, Rand. "Ted Hughes: Crow". A Companion to *Twentieth-Century Poetry.* Ed Neil Roberts. Oxford: Blackwell Publishing Ltd., 2003. 513-23. Print.

Dodsworth, Martin. "Ted Hughes and Geoffrey Hill: An Antithesis". *The Pelican Guide to English Literature 8. The Present* Ed. Boris Ford: Penguin Books, 1987. Print.

Dyson, A.E., ed. *Three Contemporary Poets.* London: Macmillan, 1990. Print.

Gifford, Terry and Neil Roberts. *Ted Hughes: A Critical Study.* London: Faber and Faber, 1981. Print.

Hughes, Ted. *Poetry in the Making.* London: Faber and Faber, 1970. Print.

Kar, P.C. "Robert Frost's 'Birches': An Oblique Statement of a Poetic Creed". *The Journal of the Department of English* 2:1, 1973-74, Utkal University, Bhubaneswar, 35-40. Print.

Larrisy, Edward. *Reading Twentieth-Century Poetry: The Language of Gender and Objects.* Oxford: Basil Blackwell Ltd., 1990. Print.

Rosenthal, M.L. *The New Poets,* New York: OUP, 1967. Print.

Sagar, Keith, ed. *The Achievement of Ted Hughes.* Manchester: Manchester University Press, 1983. Print.

Uroof, Margaret Dickie. *Sylvia Plath and Ted Hughes,* London: University of Illinois Press, 1979. Print.

Usha, V.T. *Modern English Literature.* Jaipur: Mangal Deep Publication, 1998. Print.

Williams, H.M. "English Poetry in the Fifties". *The Indian Journal of English Studies,* 4:1 (1963): 127-45. Print.

PART–II

7

Is There Such a Thing Called Canonical Criticism?

The caption of my paper is in the form of a question deliberately chosen to examine the validity of criticism and its application to literary texts. Reading of literature invites us to go into the tradition of interpretation of literature all over the world, through the ages. This prompted Valentine Cunningham to say that 'For better or worse, though, reading cannot ignore Theory, because reading can never ignore its prehistory...' (2).

Following Cunningham, Colin Davis observed that, "proper reading required a 'readerly tact' which involves not only respecting literary texts but also 'listening to what Theorists really say as well'" (165). To make the focus of my paper clear, I would like to refer to canonicity of literature. We know that there had been attempts made by the critics in the past to establish literary canon. In his well-known book, *The Western Canon,* Harold Bloom dives deep into the question of "What makes the author and the works canonical" and states that, "the answer more often than not has turned out to be strangeness, a mode of originality that either cannot be assimilated or that so assimilates us that we cease to see it as strange" (3). If for being different from other texts and also being original make a work and its writer canonical, can we say the samething about a critic and his criticism? That brings us close to the examination of the aim of the critic and the purpose of criticism.

Before explaining the business of criticism, the purpose of a critic and the reception of a reader in the act of reading a piece of literature, let us take a geometrical figure say, a rectangle or a square. The four points of a rectangle or a square, let us say, represent the author, the text, the reader and the world respectively. When the emphasis is given on one point to the exclusion of the other three (points) different kinds of criticism emerge. Upto the end of the nineteenth century in the West, the emphasis was laid on the author that gave rise to empirical criticism or biographical criticism. This is also known as romantic criticism based on the 'Author—God' concept (like God, the Author is the creator). Hence, the biography of the author was taken as a clue to interpret the work. In my paper I propose to examine the twentieth century literary criticism and find out if it is possible to accord canonical status to criticism.

In the beginning of the twentieth century T.S. Eliot, I.A. Richards and F.R. Leavis, have shifted the emphasis from the author to the text and laid an objective base for criticism. In "Tradition and the Individual Talent", Eliot said, 'To divert interest from the poet to the poetry is a laudable aim, for it would conduce to a juster estimation of actual poetry, good and bad' (*Selected Essays* 22). If this becomes the aim of the critic, then, 'Honest criticism and sensitive appreciation is directed not upon the poet but upon the poetry', (*Selected Essays* 17) asserts Eliot. If Eliot laid emphasis on the content of poetry, I.A. Richards laid emphasis on the form of poetry by laying emphasis on the use of language in literature. Both Eliot and Richards paved the way for the New Critics of America in 1940s to take centre stage by laying emphasis on the close reading of the text.

New Critics—John Crowe Ransom, Cleanth Brooks, Allen Tate, William Empson, Robert Penn Warren, William Wimsatt—each has a theory of his own. Paradox, Irony, Ambiguity, Ontology, Intentional Fallacy are the prime concern of the New Critics who espouse the cause of critical monism. They are right in making a close reading of the text and maintaining that the text has a core. But where they have erred is that they cut off the text both from the author and the reader. And what is more is that by emphasizing the autonomy of the text, they have denied inter textuality. This is a serious lapse. No wonder, the Chicago School of Critics headed by R.S. Crane reacted against the critical monism of the New Critics and pleaded for critical pluralism.

Structuralists who appeared on the critical scene in post-1950s emphasized the form and use of language in literature and thus in the hands of the Structuralists books became texts. Etymologically the text is a cloth, and 'textus' from which the text derives, means 'woven'. Like all structuralists and post-structuralists Barthes believes in multiple meaning or polysemy of interpretation. Hence, the 'Text' does not have fixity of meaning. On the other hand, it has potentiality for meaning. Barthes like other post-structuralists directs his attention primarily to how a piece of literature exemplifies the language system. In other words, he treats literature as 'Text'. It is in this sense he says that the 'Text' is plural. The 'Text' yields to plurality of meaning. In the language of a Stylistician we can say that the 'Text' has plurality of 'signification' and it is for the reader to deduce its 'value' in a given context. Roland Barthes divided the texts into two types—readerly text and writerly text. In the readerly text the reader is a passive receiver of meaning but in the writerly text, the reader re-creates the text from his point of view. That means, in the former category the text belongs to the author and while in the latter it goes into the hands of the reader. This is an erroneous judgement. It's like asking a child who does he belong to—father or mother? And as all of know that he belongs to both the parents. Similarly a text belongs to both the writer and the reader—one can't afford to ignore either.

Deconstructionists, like Structuralists are right in saying that language is not referential but self-referential. But they go a step ahead in advocating the doctrine of absence—that is, absent signs influence the meaning of the signs present. As Derrida wants us to believe that a 'chair' or 'table' is a unit, because all other units are absent from it. For not being anything else it is 'a chair' or 'a table'. This is a simplistic observation compared to I.A. Richards's 'interinanimation of words'. That is, words which are co-present in a sentence influence the meaning of each other.

Derrida is right in suggesting that writings do take place outside language. A portrait, a painting have their meanings outside language. His terms 'arche writing', 'trace', 'indeterminacy of meaning' are valid observations. Deconstructionists are right in saying that in a text there is no 'fixity' of meaning but an indeterminacy of meaning. Text is like palimpsest with layers of meaning. Key terms of deconstruction such as 'difference', 'erasure', 'trace', 'aporia', 'arche writing' are highly useful to analyse a text. But there is a difficulty in deciding who among the two, the writer and the reader deconstructs the text. Does the text get deconstructed at the time of writing? Alternatively does the text get deconstructed in the act of reading it? Deconstruction reiterates the Indian ancient view that no one can say the last word on literature. Texts are open ended.

Reader-Response Criticism lays emphasis on the act of reading and takes away the text from the author and gives it to the reader. It is true that a reader contributes to the meaning of the text by bringing his own knowledge and experience to it. He, becomes in a sense, the co-creator but to say that reader is arbitrator of the meaning of text is to miss the wood in the tree.

The text precedes the reader and survives him. A thousand readers can't alter a single line of a Shakespearean text. Reader-Response Criticism being both subjective and objective, illumines the text but it errs against proportion when it seeks to make the reader the owner of the text. The argument that meaning lies not in the text but in the mind of the reader is a brilliant example of syllogism.

But it is true that the meaning of the text depends to some extent on the interpretation of it by the reader. As readers differ, interpretations vary. Stanley Fish's observation that 'one man's reason is another man's irrelevance' (qtd. in Armstrong 19) seems to be valid.

Reading brings the subjectivity of the reader and the objectivity of the text together. The written text almost being the same for everyone, the unwritten text varies from reader to reader depending on the individual imagination. Wolfgang Iser gives one analogy to make his point clear:

> [...] two people gazing at the night sky may both be looking at the same collection of stars, but one will see

> the image of a plough and the other will make out a dipper. (57)

J. Hillis Miller in his MLA Presidential Address in 1986 underlined the course that theory has taken in the closing decades of the twentieth century in the following words:

> Literary study in the past few years has undergone a sudden, almost universal turn away from theory in the sense of an orientation toward language as such and has made a corresponding turn toward history, culture, society, politics, institution, class and gender conditions, the social context, the material base. (313)

Post-theory has different connotations. It may be taken as after theory, past theory but none of these meanings associated with the term seems to be adequate. Peter Barry makes a valid observation on the state of criticism in the following paragraph:

> Literary theory moves, not from pillar to post, but from post to post—post-structuralism, post-modernism, post-colonialism and the rest—but the post to end all posts is the widespread belief that we have been in the era of 'post theory' for more than a decade now, 'Is there life after theory?' a major UK conference wanted to know in 2003 (Derrida et al. 2004), and Eagleton's *After Theory* in the same year shows that what comes after theory might be his own version of despairing moral theology. Eagleton's book is 'post' Valentine Cunningham's *Reading After Theory* (2001), which it doesn't mention, but 'post-theory' books were around as early as 1990 when Thomas Docherty's *After Theory* was published. Yet the notion of 'after theory' as a self-contradiction, just like 'life after death' for on the one hand, if there's life after it can't be death, and on the other, if *we're* after it, it can't have been theory. Of course, theory has changed, but that doesn't mean it's dead—on the contrary. (Wolfreys 190)

Why do critics differ from each other in evaluating a text? That is because of the ideology the critics believe in. Paul B. Armstrong makes a valid observation on this aspect:

> Psychoanalysis, Marxism, phenomenology, structuralism —each has a different method of interpretation because each has a different metaphysics, a different set of convictions that makes up its point of departure and defines its position in the hermeneutic field. If an interpreter believes with Freud, for example, that human beings are sexual animals and that literary works are the disguised expression of repressed libidinal desires, he or she will arrange textual details into configurations different from those of a Marxist critic who believes that we are social, historical beings and that art reflects class interest. To embrace a type of interpretation is to make a leap of faith by accepting one set of presuppositions and rejecting others. (4-5)

Literature has 'a social dimension' and it 'exists in time and space, history and society' (52), says Michael Ryan. Its appeal to readers increases if it depicts contemporary issues. Marxist literary criticism, lays emphasis on issues that are prevalent in the society. As Michael Ryan puts it:

> Marxist literary criticism takes two major forms. The first seeks to locate literature within its social, economic, and historical context and to understand how the ideas advanced in the work of literature relate to the ideals and values that circulated in the society of the time. Such criticism tries especially to link literature to class struggle, to the conflicts between social groups that intend for economic and political power often by cultural means. A second major form of Marxist criticism consists of a critique of ideology. It seeks to understand how ideology works in literature to mask social contradictions such as those between economic groups. (53-54)

Let us take a few more schools of criticism. Feminist criticism lays emphasis on the representation of women in literature both by male and female writers. If women think that under the patriarchal system they have suffered at the hands of men, in the post-modern world and society marked by globalization, men too feel that they are overtaken by women. There is not a single position in the world such as President, Prime Minister, which has not been held by women. Women writers write now freely about sexuality and lesbianism (Manju Kapur's *A Married Women* is a case in point). Feminism gave rise to Gay and Lesbian Criticism and gender studies in the closing decades of the twentieth century. Eve Kosofsky Sedgwick's *Between Men: English Literature and Male Homo Social Desire* (1985), Judth Butler's *Bodies That Matter: On the Discursive Limits of Sex, Jane Rule's Lesbian Images* (1995), *Liltian Faderman's Surpassing the Love of Men: Romantic Friendship and Love Between Women from the Renaissance to the Present* are some of the seminal texts that popularized Gay/ Lesbian criticism. British Queer theorist Jonathan Dollimore puts Foucault's argument as follows:

> Perversion is the product and vehicle of power, a construction which enables it to gain a purchase within the realm of the Psychosexual: authority legitimates itself by fastening upon discursively constructed, sexually perverse identities of its own making. (106)

Foucault and Derrida influenced Queer Theorists in UK and USA respectively.

New Historicism's master text is Stephen Greenblatt's *The Power of Forms and Forms of Power in the Renaissance* (1982). It came as a reaction against Formalism, Structuralism and Deconstruction to re-historicize literary texts. The idea of re-historicizing the text came from Bakhtin, Foucault and Althusser. New historicists like Greenblatt, Jonathan Goldberg and Louis Advian Montrose contested the notion of 'stable point of reference' of old historicists like E.M.W. Tillyard and John Dover Wilson. Tillyard's *Elizabethan World Picture* is the master text of old historicism. The new historicists questioned the objectivity of history. As I have stated in my book, *Twentieth Century Literary Criticism*:

> The New Historicists' concept of viewing a literary text as a historical process brings to our mind Louis Montrose's comment that "the historicity of the text and the textuality of history formulate New Historicism's dialogic relation between history and literature". New Historicists discarded the concept of autonomy of the

> text, so assiduously built by the New Critics of USA in the forties who suspected history and considered it antithetical to literature. They have also rejected the Deconstructionists' notion of literature as a kind of 'free play' without a centre and tried to bring a kind of understanding between two extreme positions held by the New Critics on the one hand and the Deconstructionists on the other. (Das 125)

Criticism has taken a trajectory path by moving from ideas and concepts to language and then to culture, which is now considered as the source of literature. Therefore, Cultural Criticism became a favourite tool with the critics. Raymond Williams's term 'Cultural Materialism,' Stephen Greenblatt's term 'Cultural Poetics' and Mikhail Bakhtin's term, 'Cultural Prosaics' have become significant in the field of Cultural Studies and Cultural Criticism. Here, I would like to make a reference to my earlier observation in the follow words:

> In 1970s there is a shift in emphasis as literary critics started discussing cultural criticism in terms of 'hegemony' under the influence of Italian Marxist, Antonio Gramsci. With the arrival of Louis Althusser and Jacques Lacan on the literary and cultural field, the structuralist mode of cultural criticism got intersected with ideological approach of Althusser and Psychoanalytic framework of Lacan. If Hoggart, Williams and Hall gave one direction to culture studies and cultural criticism in the 1950s, and after in 1970s Gramsci, Althusser and Lacan gave another direction for exploring literary studies within the ambit of a given culture in the social context in which the text is produced. (Das 405)

Postcolonial criticism, springs from post-colonialism associated with the colonial power and the colonized subjects. Bill Ashcroft, Gareth Griffiths and Helen Tiffin in their well-known book titled *Postcolonial Studies: Key Concepts* explained the term post-colonialism in the following words:

> Post-colonialism (or often post-colonialism) deals with the effects of colonization on cultures and societies. As

> originally used by historians after the second world war in terms such as the post-colonial state, 'post-colonial' had a clearly chronological meaning, designating the post-independence period. However, from the late 1970s the term has been used by literary Critics to discuss the various cultural effects of colonization. (186)

Postcolonial criticism owes its origin to Frantz Fanon, Mahatma Gandhi, Edward Said, Gayatri Spivak Chakravorty and Homi K. Bhabha. It deals with politics, ideology, identity, migration, alternative histories and leads to neo-colonialism. Political imperialism of the colonial period is replaced by economic imperialism of the neo-colonial era. Above all, postcolonial criticism is politico-social criticism.

The term post-theory is not past theory and after theory is not the absence of theory. 'Post' may mean a transition from one school of theory to another. For instance, We say, structuralism/post-structuralism, feminism/post-feminism, colonialism/post-colonialism modernism/post-modernism, and so on. Literature is read and will continue to be read in terms of a theoretical framework. *In Conflicting Readings: Variety and Validity in Interpretation,* Paul B. Armstrong has rightly stated:

> The literary work is not autonomous but "heteronomous". While a work transcends any individual interpretation, it exits only in and through its concretizations—so much so that it will cease to exist in any meaningful sense if it is no longer read. (11)

Literary criticism is the product of collective endeavour. Therefore, it is heterogenous, and pluralistic in nature. Since a literary text is built on several texts, it admits of inter textuality. The foundation of a text is explained by an anecdote by Paul B. Armstrong in the following words:

> This state of affairs recalls the well-known story of the man who tells the philosopher that the world is supported on the back of a turtle. When the Philosopher asks him what holds up the turtle, the man replies, 'Another turtle'. When asked what the turtle stands on, he answers with some exasperation, 'Sir, it's turtles all the way down'.

> The quest for foundations invariably leads ad infinitum to ever more foundation. (153)

We know that literary texts have achieved canonical status by surving the death of the authors for generations. Similarly some writers have achieved canonical status through their works. In the words of Harold Bloom, "Canonical Prophecy needs to be tested about two generations after a writer dies" (522). We have a number of English authors that have stood this test successfully.

Literary theory/criticism unlike literature run the risk of being contested by other schools of theory/criticism quickly. We find between 1960s and 1980s there is a plethora of theories—Structuralism, Deconstruction Marxist Criticism, Reader-Response Criticism, Cultural Criticism, Feminist Criticism, New Historicism, Queer Theory and Post-Colonial Criticism. Each school is based on an Ideology and therefore, evoked resentment.

Each school of criticism has some validity though limited and is applicable to some texts. That is because no school of criticism is comprehensive enough to apply to all literary texts. Texts always elude criticism by its capacity to be interpreted by different schools of criticism at the sametime. The focus of criticism is limited but not all pervasive. For instance, in Psychoanalytic criticism we take the subconscious mind as vital, overlooking the fact that though man has a subconscious mind, he is not a subconscious mind. In Queer Theory we argue with Judith Butler that bodies matter 'on the discursive limits of sex'. Our fate lies in the body, argue the queer theorists but they tend to forget that we have a mind too (not to speak of the soul). Sex and sexuality are a part of life but not the whole of it.

To conclude, I should say that literary criticism in the last thirty years (i.e., post-1980) ceases to be literary. It has become part of culture studies and social criticism. Cultural theory and social critical thought now continue to dominate literary studies. It is a serious loss. The theory now does not seek to distinguish between literature and non-literature. The emphasis has now shifted from examining the literariness of the text to the factors that have gone into the making of the text. The border line between literature and non-literature seems to be blurred. Hence, criticism can't be canonized the way literature is canonized. However, criticism will continue to influence our reading of literature. We may call it 'post-theory', 'death of theory' 'after theory' or by any other name. Theory will survive and influence interpretation. But 'theory' will continue to be contested by other theories (old and new). On the other hand, some critics will be remembered for setting the trends in literary criticism in the twentieth century. T.S. Eliot, I.A. Richards, F.R. Leavis, Cleanth Brooks, Roland Barthes, Jacques Derrida, Stanley Fish, Jonalthan Culler, Stephen Greenblatt, Raymond Williams, Antonio Gramsci, Louis Althusser, Jacques Lacan, Edward Said, Homi K. Bhabha and Gayatri Spivak Chakravorty will continue to influence literary theory and criticism in the years to come. But criticism however objective it may be, will always remain an academic exercise. It will exist only as a satellite of literature to enhance the communication between the text and the reader. Individual schools of criticism may come and go but criticism as a tool of evaluation of literature will remain. We may say that criticism is dead, long live criticism! That's the beauty of criticism.

WORKS CITED

Armstrong, Paul B. *Conflicting Readings.* London: The University of North Carolina Press, 1990. Print.

Ashcroft, Bill, et al. *Postcotonial Studies: The Key Concepts.* London: Routledge, 1998 rpt. 2004. Print.

Barry, Peter. "The Development of Literary Theory Since 1995". *Modern British and Irish Criticism and Theory: A Critical Guide.* Ed. Julian Wolfreys. Edinburgh: Edinburgh University Press Ltd., 2006. Print.

Bloom, Harold. *The Western Canon: The Books and School of Ages.* London: MacMillan, 1995. Print.

Cunningham, Valentine. *Reading After Theory.* Massachusetts: Blackwell Publishers Inc, 2002. Print.

Das, Bijay Kumar. *Twentieth Century Literary Criticism* (6th edn.). New Delhi: Atlantic Publishers, 2010. Print.

Davis, Colin. *After Poststructuralist: Reading, Stories and Theory.* London: Routledge, 2004. Print.

Dollimore, Jonathan. *Sexual Dissidence: Augustine to Wilde, Freud to Foucault.* Oxford: OUP, 1991. Print.

Eliot, T.S. *Selected Essays.* London: Faber and Faber, 1951. Print.

Iser, Wolfgang. "The Reading Process: A Phenomenological Approach". *Reader-Response Criticism.* Ed. Jane P. Tompkins. Baltimore: The Johns Hopkins University Press, 1980. Print.

Miller, J. Hillis. "Presidential Address: The Triumph of Theory, the Resistance to Reading, and the Question of the Material Base". *Theory Now and Then.* Durham: NC, 1991. Print.

Ryan, Michael. *Literary Theory: A Practical Introduction.* Oxford: Blackwell Publishers Ltd., 2001. Print.

8

Interrogating the Theories about the Author and the Text

The difference between the Author and the writer is a matter of nuance. It is simplistic to say that the author is the owner of the text and the writer is the scriptor of it. Similarly, the difference between the work and the text is more a matter of perception, convenience than an empirical reality. Theories have been built around the author and the text from the Romantic age to the present time (i.e. 2013). Schools of Criticism like Formalism (both American and Russian varieties), Structuralism, Reader-Response Criticism, New Historicism and Postcolonialism have examined the question of authorship and textuality from various angles. The purpose of this paper is to show that most of the critics belonging to these schools of criticism have lost sight of the enormity of the authorship and the validity of the text vis-a-vis the response of the reader. Moreover, literature being what it is, no theory can overtake it, let alone interpret it definitively.

Andrew Bennett while examining the importance of Author throughout the ages refers to Sean Burke's observation, "'there is no theory of literature or the text which does not imply a certain stance' towards the author (Burke IX). Debates over authorship have been particularly intense in criticism and theory during the last two centuries, and especially over the last fifty years. Literary theory, we might say, is largely a question of author theory" (Bennett 4). In his "Preface" to the *Lyrical Ballads* (1802) Wordsworth asks, "what is meant by the word Poet? What is a Poet? To whom does he address himself? And what language is to be expected from him?" And then goes on to say that, "he is a man speaking to men: a man it is true, endowed with more lively sensibility, more enthusiasm and tenderness, who has a greater knowledge of human nature and a more comprehensive soul..." (Enright and Chickera 171). Coleridge has an answer to Wordsworth's questions in his famous work, *Biographia Literaria* (1817):

> 'What is poetry?' is so nearly the same question with, what is a poet?', declares Coleridge, 'that the answer to the one is involved in the solution of the other'. (qtd. in Bennet 3)

The poet is a creator and he has also inwardness with human nature. That is why, the Romantics lay emphasis on the poet and give him an exalted position, Author becomes God as a creator.

Let us take a few lines from Barthes's "The Death of the Author" in order to understand his view point and then contest some of his untenable ideas. Here are a few extracts:

1. For him (Mallarme), for us too, it is language which speaks, not the author, to write is, through a prerequisite impersonality, to reach that point, where the language acts, 'performs' and not 'me' (Rice and Waugh 186).
2. Linguistically, the author is never more than the instance writing, just as I is nothing other than the instance saying I: language knows a 'subject' and not a 'person' ... (Rice and Waugh 187).
3. The Author, when believed in is always conceived of as the past of his own book: book and author stand automatically on a single line divided into a 'before' and an 'after' (Rice and Waugh 187).
4. We know that a text is now a line of words releasing a single theological meaning (the 'message' of the Author-God) but a multidimensional space in which a variety of writings none of them original, blend and clash. The text is a tissue of quotations drawn from the innumerable centres of culture (Rice and Waugh 188).
5. Once the Author is removed, the claim to decipher a text becomes quite futile. To give a text an Author is to impose

> a limit on that text, to furnish it with a final signified, to close the writing. Such a conception suits criticism very well, the latter then allotting itself the important task of discovering the Author, beneath the work, when the Author has been found, the text is 'explained'—victory to the critic (Rice and Waugh 188).

Let us examine the basis of Barthes's observations. For the structuralists including Barthes the form is the content. Language is a system of signs which existed much before the Author takes it for use. Words have a lot of associations, figurations and are used by many predecessors of the Author. Hence, when the Author uses the words he begins to speak the voices of his ancestors and follows 'other echoes in the garden' (Eliot's coinage in *Four Quartets*). But Barthes forgets that like a skilful navigator the Author sails in the sea of words and arrives at the shore (i.e., says what he means to say). No doubt, he says in words but 'words obey his call',—words don't master him, he masters them.

Coming to the second point we recall Heidegger's words, 'language speaks not man', in which Barthes' observation that Author is 'an instance of writing' and language knows 'a subject' not a person is foregrounded. Barthes, misses the wood in the tree. Man is the user of language but great writers are not only the users of it but the creators as well. Linguistics admits of neologism (nonce formation). Language is the tool in the hands of writers (I am using here the word 'writer' as a synonym of 'Author' not being oblivious of the subtle differences between them, which I will state towards the end of this paper). Language does not write but is made to write in the hands of the writer.

In the third quotation Barthes admits willy nilly that Author is the conceiver of the text (work/book) and therefore, the book owes its conception to the Author. Inadvertently Barthes makes a mistake by stating that "book and author stand automatically on a single line divided into a 'before' and an 'after'." It should have been author and book stand automatically on a single line divided into a 'before' and an 'after'.

Barthes is absolutely right in admitting intertextuality, 'a tissue of quotations drawn from innumerable centres of culture', as a base for the writing of texts by the Author. Author may not be highly original and self-sufficient in knowledge. Knowledge is derived from several sources: reading, experiencing and seeking. But it is the Author who acquires knowledge—not vice versa (knowledge does not acquire the Author). Language is a medium, but author is the user of that medium. It is a travesty of truth to say that the medium controls the user. Author is not only the owner of the text but the weaver of words 'stich by stich'.

Barthes's claim to remove the Author from the text is partially true. That is because oral texts do not have authors, so also myths. They are handed down from generation to generation in terms of tales being told by the tellers to the listeners. Neither the authenticity of these texts is questioned nor the authorship is being looked into. They are taken as they are, accepted by people from generation to generation. But such is not the case with written texts. Here authorship is known—individual writers, corporate Authors and sometimes groups of translators as is the case of *The Authorized Version of the Bible.*

Let me turn to Michel Foucault's "What Is an Author?" Foucault contests Barthes's claim of the disappearance of the author by bringing into question the status of a work. He writes:

> A certain number of notions that are intended to replace the privileged position of the author actually seem to preserve that privilege and suppress the real meaning of his disappearance.... At this point, however, a problem arises: what is a work? What is this curious unity which we designate as a work? Of what elements is it composed? Is it not what an author has written? Difficulties appear immediately. If an individual were not an author, could we say that what he wrote, said, left behind in his papers, or what has been collected of his remarks, could be called a "work"? (Rabinow 103)
>
> Foucault further adds: Texts, books and discourses really began to have authors (other than mythical, "sacralized" and "sacralizing" figures) to the extent that authors became subject to punishment, that is, to the extent that discourses could be transgressive. (Rabinow 108)

Foucault takes a dig at Barthes when he says,

> It is not enough, however to repeat the empty affirmation that the author has disappeared. For the same reason, it is now enough to keep repeating (after Nietzche) that God and man have died a common death. Instead, we must locate the space left empty by the author's disappearance, follow the distribution of gaps and breaches, and watch for the openings that this disappearance uncovers (Rabinow 105).

What Foucault says in not so many words is that Author is the unity of his work. Author is economically the owner of the work and the work is his property. Royalty of the work is due to him and copyright is mostly vested in him. About writing a work or say, a text, the Author may borrow plots, characters, incidents, situations from other texts and build his text on them. Let us take the example of two great authors, Shakespeare and Eliot from English literature. Both of them have borrowed from several sources (Shakespeare's plays and Eliot's well-known poems, *The Waste Land* and *Four Quartets* are full of literary borrowings from the East and the West). But what is important is not the borrowings but what they did with the borrowings. Shakespeare borrowed skeletons but put blood and flesh into them and the result is that we got lively plays which 'time cannot wither away nor custom stale'. Shakespeare became the unity of his work. A thousand readers cannot alter a single line of a Shakespearean text. Similarly, Eliot who brought everyday conversational language into the realms of poetry placed us all in his debt by influencing the modern poets in the English speaking world in the twentieth century. Nearer home, we have several Authors of the *Ramayana* and the *Mahabharata* in respective regional literatures of our country (I would desist from using G.N. Devy's term 'Bhasha literatures', for the single reason that it is a misnomer. If in our country bhasha means language, all literatures are written in languages, and therefore, all literatures should be termed bhasha literatuers—why not treat Indian English literature as a bhasha literature?). These Authors have transcreated Valmiki's *Ramayana* and Vyasa's *Mahabharata* into their respective languages and we take their works as original.

Foucault after successfully contesting Barthes's notion of the author, errs in another direction. He writes:

> We are accustomed, as we have seen earlier, to saying that the author is the general creator of a work, in which he deposits, with infinite wealth and generosity, an inexhaustible world of significations.... The truth is quite the contrary: the author is not an indefinite source of significations which fill a work, the author does not precede the works.... One can say that he author is an ideological product...the ideological figure by which one marks the manner in which we fear the proliferation of meaning (Rabinow 118-19).

The Author may not precede the works (i.e. the works by his predecessors), but he surely precedes his own work. Secondly all the Authors are not ideological figures. What about the first Authors/Writers in a language? Who influenced them? What about the born blind poets? Say for instance, the likes of Bhima Bhoi, a born blind Odia poet.

Foucault's essay, "What Is an Author?" begins with Beckett's statement, "What does it matter who is speaking"—the indifference is loudly pronounced. And Foucault ends his essay with an interrogation: "What difference does it make who is speaking?" Foucault moves from indifference to cynicism, which is unfortunate. The concluding interrogation hints at the unoriginality of the Author. Everything, as it were, had been said before. Far from true. "In trying to learn the use of words, every attempt is a wholly new start and a different kind of failure" says Eliot. Rightly so. The Author is not always derivative in approach as well as technique. He also innovates as he writes and produces a text.

In an essay, "The Author as Producer" (taken from *Understanding Brecht* translated by Anna Bostock 1973), Walter Benjamin reiterates the following points:

> The crucial point, therefore, is that a writer's production must have the character of a model: it must be able to instruct other writers in their production and, secondly, it must be able to place an improved apparatus at their disposal. The apparatus will be better, the more

> consumers it brings into contact with the production process—in short, the more readers or spectators it turns into collaborators. (Newton 170)

Margaret Atwood in her book, *Negotiating with the Dead: A Writer on Writing* explains the problems faced by the writers and seeks to solve them as far as she can. She writes:

> There are the three questions most often posed by readers and by themselves: Who are you writing for? Why do you do it? Where does it come from? (xix)

These three searching questions cover the intention of the author, the implied reader, and the source of his/her writing. They inevitably bring into focus the relation between the Author and the reader vis-a-vis the work (text), from the making of it to its evaluation. The intention of the Author is neither available to the reader, nor is it desirable to know. (William K. Wimsatt and Monroe C. Beardsley's essay "The Intentional Fallacy" (1946) is well known.) The implied reader, a term coined by a Reader-Response Critic, Wolfgang Iser stands as a contrast to the actual reader.

> Whereas the actual reader could be any individual who happens to have read or to be reading the text, the implied reader is the reader intended, even created by the text. Iser calls this reader a 'construct' of the text who embodies all those predispositions necessary for a literary work to exercise its effect. (Murfin and Ray 171)

Wayne C. Booth in *Rhetoric of Fiction* (1961) uses the term 'implied author' to "refer to the unique and pervasive human presence that the reader senses is the driving force behind a literary work.... As Booth puts it, the implied author is an, 'ideal, literary, created version', of the real author. In a sense, the implied author is the character or persona that the real author creates to represent, himself or herself to the reader" (Murfin and Ray 171).

Speaking about the purpose behind writing we have an author lexicon such as, "Apparitional author, Author-construct, Author function, Historical author, Implied author, Scriptor, Created author, Romantic author, Writer" (Bennett 128). The list is endless and misleading—stretching the meaning of the 'Author' too far. It is better to stick to the textual author (who actually writes the text) and the textual reader (who actually reads it) to understand the identity of the Author and the validity of the text properly.

I am inclined to agree with Susan Onega and Jose Angel Gracia Landa's view point:

> The textual author is a virtual image of the author's attitudes, as presented by the text. The textual reader is a virtual receiver created by the author in full view of the actual audience he or she presumes for his or her work. The textual reader need not coincide with the author's conception of the audience: this reader figure may be a rhetorical strategy, a role which the author wishes the audience to assume (or even to reject). (9)

The structuralists sought to downplay the importance of the Author by overplaying the use of language in literature. The deconstructionists lead by Jacques Derrida maintained that the text is a 'free play of signifiers without a centre'. For them 'indeterminancy of meaning' became the hall mark of literature. Derrida coined the term 'Human Sciences' for literature and social sciences put together. The reason is that both literature and social sciences use metaphorical language instead of literal language. For structuralists and post-structuralists work or book became a text. Literature like Political Science, Sociology, etc. is a text. This is a serious loss for literature to be evaluated in terms of social sciences. Reader-Response Critics shifted the emphasis from the Author to the Reader. Stanley Fish's *Is There a Text in this Class?* is a death blow to the text and an indirect denial of the importance of the author. Can we ask here, if the text is not there, where will the reader's response come from? Rhetorically a text becomes a text only if there is a reader otherwise not, in the same way as 'if a tree falls in the forest and nobody hears it, does it make a sound?' 'Meaning lies not in the text but in the minds of the reader,' say the Reader-Response Critics. These kinds of arguments are fallacious.

Marxist critics speak of the role of class consciousness and ideology in the creation of the texts. Texts are not created on the basis of ideology but they reveal ideological positions. Similarly women writers resent authorship with 'patriarchal heritage' and in the words of Helene Cixous, woman 'must write herself' and 'put herself into the text' (347).

There are innumerable theories about the text. In S/2 (1970) Roland Barthes speaks of two types of texts: 'lisible' (readerly), which evokes a passive response from the reader. As a contrast to this, 'scritible' text (writerly text) invites and prompts the reader to interpret in his own way. In interpreting it, the reader is said to re-write it. This idea is untenable, for all texts are received or interpreted by the reader. The reader while deducing the meaning from the text, thinks of both the Author and the text. Even when the Author's name is not there, the reader evokes the implied author. Text is having both filiative and affiliative relationship with the Author and the World (Vico's idea) respectively. That led Edward Said to say that the text is in the world and about the world and hence 'worldly'.

To conclude, let me say that the identity of the Author either visible or invisible is established by the text. The person who unravels it is not the Author but the reader, vis-a-vis the text (work). No theory of literature can do away with the Author, as it cannot abandon the text or disown the reader. The Author enters the text as a character—the examples of Valmiki and Vyasa stare us in our face. On the other hand, for the reader "a book (text) is another country. You enter it, but then you must leave: like the Underworld, you can't live there" (Atwood 173). As the reader cannot live in the text forever, he can't drive away the Author from there. Between the Author and the reader, the text is exquisitely balanced owing its meaning to both of them.

WORKS CITED

Atwood, Margaret. *Negotiating with the Dead: A Writer on Writing.* Cambridge University Press, 2002. Print.

Barthes, Roland. "The Death of the Author". *Modern Literary Theory.* Eds. Philip Rice and Patricia Waugh. London: Arnold, 2002. Print.

Benjamin, Walter. "The Author as Producer". *Twentieth Century Literary Theory: A Reader.* Ed. K.M. Newton. London: MacMillan Press Ltd., 1997. Print.

Bennett, Andrew. *The Author,* New York: Routledge, 2005. Print.

Burke, Sean, ed. *Authorship: From Plato to Postmodernism: A Reader.* Edinburgh: Edinburgh University Press, 1995. Print.

Cixous, Helene. “The Laugh of the Medusa”. *Feminisms: An Anthology of Literary Theory and Criticism.* Eds. Robyn R. Warhol and Diane Price Herndl. Basingstoke: MacMillan, 1997. Print.

Foucault, Michel. “What Is an Author?” *The Foucault Reader.* Ed. Paul Rabinow. New York Pantheon Books, 1984. Print.

Murfin, Ross and Supriya M. Ray. *The Bedford Glossary of Critical and Literary Terms.* London: MacMillan Press Ltd., 1998. Print.

Onega, Susan and Jose Angel Gracia Landa, eds. *Narratology.* Harlow: Longman, 1996. Print.

Wordsworth, William. “Preface to Lyrical Ballads”. *English Critical Texts.* Eds. D.J. Enright and Ernst De Chickera, Kolkata: OUP, 2001. Print.

9

Theorizing Poetry: Sri Aurobindo, Nissim Ezekiel, and A.K. Ramanujan as Critics

Theorizing poetry involves the source and nature of poetry, the nationality of the poet, the tradition and culture to which he/she belongs, his/her knowledge and belief and above all the art of writing poetry. It is not easy to define poetry in clear cut terms, because it is as elusive as God. No wonder epic poetry begins with an invocation to the Muse or Deity. Different kinds of poetry make different kinds of demands on the poets—all these have different stanzas, language and vocabulary with which we are familiar. Similarly, age wise, we have Romantic poetry, Classical poetry, Modern poetry and so on. How to theorize poetry? This brings to our mind, T.S. Eliot's essay, "Tradition and the Individual Talent". A poet learns from tradition and extends it by his individual talent and experience. This is what Eliot wants us to believe in the greatness of a poet. Sri Aurobindo, too works in this line in his *Future Poetry.*

Nationality of the poet and the age to which he belongs are important factors in the making of his poetry. What gives identity to poetry and for that matter to literature is not language but nationality. W.B. Yeats emphatically states it in his poem "Under Ben Bullben":

> Many times man lives and dies
> Between his two eternities
> That of race and that of soul
> And Ancient Ireland knew it all.

R. Parthasarathy reiterates it in his *Rough Passage*, giving as it were, a clarion call to Indian poets to go back to their roots. He writes:

> How long can foreign poets
> provide the staple of your lines?
> Turn inward. Scrape the bottom of your past.
> ("Homecoming 2")

Derek Walcott, the Caribbean Nobel Laureate who had a dilemma to choose between Africa (the land of his ancestors) and America, the place of his work and current stay concludes his poem, "A Far Cry from Africa" with the line, "How can I turn from Africa and live?" It is further reinforced in *Omeros* when says that "either I'm nobody or I'm nation."

No theory of poetry can afford to ignore the poet no matter what the Reader-Response Critics, Structuralists, Deconstructionists, and Cultural Critics say about the eclipse of the author. Let me turn to Sri Aurobindo to assess his views on poetry and poet as stated in his *The Future Poetry.* Sri Aurobindo writes:

> The work of the poet depends not only on himself and his age but on the mentality of the nation to which he belongs and the spiritual, intellectual, aesthetic tradition and environment which it creates for him. (38)

Sri Aurobindo speaks in the same way about the dual personality of the poet as T.S. Eliot does in his critical essays. To Eliot the poet has an empirical personality (i.e., the poet as a person) and an implied personality (i.e., the point of view embodies in his work). Sri Aurobindo states:

> The poet has in him a double personality, a double instrument of his responses to life and existence. There is in him the normal man absorbed in mere living who thinks and feels and acts like others, and there is a seer of things, the supernormal man, the super-soul, or delight-soul in touch with the impersonal and eternal fountains of joy and beauty who creates from that source and transmutes by its alchemy all experience into a form of the spirits of Ananda. (*The Future Poetry* 241)

If Eliot says that what the poet expresses is not his personality but 'a particular medium' ("Tradition and the Individual Talent"), and the structuralist follow Heidegger's dictum, "language writes the man", Aurobindo opines:

> A poet or artist may be a medium for creative force which uses him as a channel and is concerned only with expression in art and not with the man's personality or his inner or outer life. He is a medium for the creative force which acts through him; it uses or picks up anything stored up in his mind from his inner life or his memories or impressions of outer life and things, anything it can and cares to make use of and this is moulds and turns to its purpose. (*The Future Poetry* 328)

In "The Sources of Poetry" Sri Aurobindo states that poetry is not "a creation but rather the revelation of something that eternally exists. The ancients knew this truth and used the same word for poet and prophet, creator and seer, sophos, vates, kavi" (Devy 154). To Aurobindo the poet is 'seer,' 'Kavi' and even 'Rishi'. He believes that "the great poet interprets to man his present or reinterprets for him his past but can also point him to his future and in all three reveal to him the face of the Eternal" (*The Future Poetry* 203). The only critic in the west of his time who can be compared with Sri Aurobindo is T.S. Eliot. Like Eliot, Sri Aurobindo is a poet-critic (that to an epic poet) and a polyglot who knew several languages like English French, Italian, Bengali, Gujarati and above all Sanskrit. Like Eliot, Sri Aurobindo has not thought much of British Romantic poets. He writes:

> Shelley, Keats and Wordsworth have not been brought into consideration although their best work is as fine poetry as any written but they have written nothing on a larger scale which would place them among the greatest creators. If Keats had finished *Hyperion* (without spoiling it), if Shelley had lived and Wordsworth had not petered out like a motor car with insufficient petrol, it might be different, but we have to take things as they are. (*The Future Poetry* 521-52)

Aurobindo believes in divine inspiration, speaks of poetry as a utterance of the universal soul.

India's foremost poet in the English language, Nissim Ezekiel is a poet-critic, the fourth category of critics Eliot extols in his well-known essay, "To Criticize the Critic". Ezekiel's criticism is contained in his well-known book titled, *Selected Prose*. His seminar critical essays include, "How a Poem is Written", "To Revise or not to Revise", "Poetry as Knowledge", "Poetry and Philosophy" and "Philosophy of the Literary Man". As is well-known poetry is usually written in one of the two says: under inspiration, divine or human or by reading others' poetry and making an effort for it. Ezekiel believes in the second method and says, "Poetry begets poetry. Reading poems, some people write them" (*Selected Prose* 11). He refers to Osip Mandelstam and W.B. Yeats to explain how a poem can be written in both ways.

Ezekiel writes:

> The wife of Russian poet Mandelstam avows that he composed the entire poem in his head before he dictated it to her, and that he revised very little, if at all. Both the happiness and the suffering of the poet as poet were derived from the utter dependence on a wholly unpredictable visitation in which words, phrases, lines, stanzas, and finally complete poems arranged themselves, so to speak, and achieved form without that struggle on the page, with a writing instrument that is, for most writers, the crucial act of writing. Mandelstam did not write, in that sense, he was written.... (*Selected Prose* 14-15)

Here Ezekiel is with Sri Aurobindo and the structuralists, reinforcing Heidegger's statement quoted earlier in the paper. Again Ezekiel goes on to analyse W.B. Yeats's view that poetry is written with zeal and great effort by revision after revision. He quotes the following lines from Yeats's poem to bring home his point:

> A line will take us hours, maybe,
> Yet, if it does not seem a moment's thought,
> Our stitching and unstitching has been nought.
>
> ("Adam's Curse")

Ezekiel refers to the works of Paul Valery, T.S. Eliot and Rilke to say that poetry is written either by hard work like reading or by waiting for it to happen. In his poem, "Poet, Lover, Bird Watcher" he says emphatically, "The best poets wait for words."

In his essay, "To Revise or not to Revise" foregrounded in Hamlet's famous speech 'To be or not to be, that is the question." Ezekiel like most of the modern poets opines in favour of revision. But he asserts that though revision is necessary it is not always obligatory. Here are two examples from his own experience:

> Revision means raising the uninspired sections, after recognizing them as uninspired, to the level of the inspired bits or cutting them out. I once had an experience with the help of A.K. Ramanujan which taught me to cope with such poems. It was in 1967 in Chicago, where I was his guest, using part of the available time preparing a few lectures and the rest to revise a batch of poems I had taken along. I was very pleased when Ramanujan picked up one of my poems from the batch on my table and said it was inspired. Immediately afterwards he shocked me by saying, 'If you cut out the first nine lines and the last fourteen lines, this will be a good poem'. I stammered something to the effect that since the poem had only 35 lines in it, cutting out 23 would leave only 12. 'Yes', he replied, 'but those 12 lines are the inspired ones. If you want it to be a longer poem, you can revise some or all of the other 23.' Eventually, I cut some and revised others, making it a poem of 19 lines. Later, I rewrote the hard core of the poem, restructuring the metrical phrases into vertical one-word two-word lines, virtually the only poem of its kind I have written. (*Selected Prose* 23-24)

Again he cites from his own experience how he wrote "Night of the Scorpion":

> I decided to spend the day in my University room waiting, in Rilke's sense, for a poem, with only one proviso: it had to be Indian. My wife and I settled down in that room around 10 a.m.; by lunch-time I had had no luck, by tea-time none either. Eventually, when my wife warned

> me that it was approaching 6 p.m. and that we would soon have to leave for the party, I wrote down in a fit of desperation and after making a joke about the words 'I remember', the joke being 'I remember, I remember the house where I was born', then, suddenly I wrote, 'the night my mother was stung by a scorpion' and, in as much time as it would take to make a copy of the poem, I had completed it. (*Selected Prose* 24)

Later on when he sent the poem for publication, he made "an extra space between the body of the poem and the last three lines". In case of revision, the poet should take extra care to improve upon the earlier draft—not to spoil the poem. Ezekiel refers to Yeats, Dylan Thomas, W.H. Auden to show the importance of revision before publication of the poem. He also quotes Robert Lowell who said that poetry "is a craft, purely a craft and there must be some break through back into life" (*Selected Prose* 27).

In "Poetry as Knowledge", Ezekiel makes a practical analysis of Wordsworth's "The Solitary Reaper" disagrees with C. Day-Lewis's analysis of this poem, by saying, "knowledge of a mood is no knowledge at all".... He also questions I.A. Richards's observations on poetry as 'Pseudo-statements'.

> To describe the statements of poetry as pseudo-statements, which I.A. Richards does, is to devalue poetry, even if unintentionally, in relation to the statements of science, accepting the latter as providing the norm. The distinction between the two types of statements in terms of true and pseudo is deplorable because poetry is true or nothing, though its mode of approaching, grasping, and expressing the truth may be different from that of science. Poetic truth is not pseudo-truth, if such a term is permissible. (*Selected Prose* 34)

Knowledge is assimilated in poetry through emotion and, 'What the poet knows makes the poem what it is...' says Ezekiel and rightly so. Ezekiel's criticism is born out of his knowledge as a poet and poetry editor. What he speaks about his own way of writing poetry applies to other poets as well. Ezekiel proves Eliot right when the latter prefers poet-critics to all other critics.

A.K. Ramanujan though a poet-critic, his eminence lies in being a postcolonial critic. If Edward Said speaks of 'Orientalism', Bhabha 'hybridity', Gayatri Spivak 'catachreism', Ramanujan emphasizes on excavating indigenous and alternative history to challenge the hegemony of former colonizers. Like Jawaharlal Nehru who favoured the retention of English in our country, Ramanujan underlines the importance of English as a second language in our country. In course of an interview given to A.L. Becker and Keith Taylor, Ramanujan says:

> English has distorted our traditions, but it has also made us look at our traditions. It's not enough to say that it is all colonialism and has done nothing but distort. This whole question of colonial distortion has been formulated in English. It requires a dialogue with English. English has been the 'other' through which we have returned to ourselves. English has become a part of us. To say we want to return to a pre-English state is chimerical. The anti-colonial discourse is all done in English. Nobody's writing this in Kannada. In India, there is a wonderful group of new historians called the Subalterns, who are looking at all the distortions of the colonial intellectual practices. But all their work is done in English. Isn't the English in which they are writing distorting shat they are writing about? English has made us self-critical and made us critical of English itself. (Daniels-Ramanujan and Keith Harrison 79)

It is through English we have discovered our past and ancient literature. Numerous translations of Bhasha Literatures into English helped us to discover the nation. Ramanujan's translation of Tamil poets into English and U.R. Anantha Murthy's *Samskara* into English speaks volumes for Ramanujan's effort to bring indigenous Indian literature to the notice of Anglo-American readers and writers. "Is there an Indian way of Thinking?" show how intertextuality which is being talked of in the west now, was there in India from immemorial. Indian literature is context-sensitive. Ramanujan observes:

> No Indian text comes without a context, a frame, till the nineteenth century. Works are framed by *phalasruti*

> verses—these verses tell the reader, reciter or listener all the good that will result from his act of reading, reciting or listening. They relate the text, or whatever antiquity, to the present reader—that is, they contextualize it. (Dharwadker 41-42)

Ramanujan brings to our notice the art of story telling and context sensitive Indian literary texts by giving examples from the *Mahabharata*. Our epics and puranas begin in reference to earlier texts. He observes:

> The *Ramayana* and *Mahabharata* open with episodes that tell you why and under what circumstances they were composed. Every such story is encased in a meta-story. And within the text, one tale is the context for another within it; not only does the outer frame-story motivate the inner sub-story; the inner story illuminates the outer as well. It often acts as a microcosmic replica for the whole text. In the forest when the Pandava brothers are in exile, the eldest, Yudhisthira, is in the very slough of despondency: he has gambled away a kingdom, and is in exile. In the depth of his despair, a sage visits him and tells him the story of Nala. As the story unfolds, we see Nala too gamble away a kingdom, lose his wife, wander in the forest, and finally, win his wager, defeat his brother reunite with his wife and return to his kingdom. Yudhisthira, following the full curve of Nala's adventures, sees that he is only halfway through his own, and sees his present in perspective, himself as a story yet to be finished. Very often the Nala story is excerpted and read by itself, but its poignancy is partly in its frame, its meaning for the hearer within the fiction and for the listener of the whole epic. The tale within is context-sensitive—getting its meaning from the tale without, and giving it further meanings. (Dharwadker 42)

Ramanujan's originality lies in interpreting Indian literature by going to the roots—that is, resituating the text in the context. That is what, new historicists seek to do in the west. He paves the way for modern interpretation of ancient Tamil poetics in his seminal essay, "On Ancient Tamil Poetics." He writes:

> Akam and Puram are ancient, complex words. To understand them is to enter Tamil poetics, and much that is crucial to Tamil culture. According to *A Dravidian Etymological Dictionary,* they are also current in all the South Dravidian languages and in Telugu and Tulu. In classical poetry, as we have seen, *akam* poems are love poems; *puram* are all other kinds of poems, usually about war, values, community; it is the 'public' poetry of the ancient Tamils, celebrating the ferocity and glory of kings, lamenting the death of heroes, the poverty of poets. Elegies, panegyrics, invectives, poems on wars and tragic events are *puram* poems. (Devy 346-47)

Ramanujan has inwardness with Dravidian literature and his interpretation of ancient texts bears the stamp of originality. He uses tropes such as metaphor and metonymy to bring out the distinction between man and woman as they are portrayed in Tamil poetry. The concluding lines of his essays, "On Ancient Tamil Poetics" illustrate Ramanujan insight into Tamil literature. He writes:

> In many *akam* poems, a woman's body is suggestively present to our senses—the smell or texture of her hair, the shape of her breast, her brow, her mound of love or black-snake pubis, her leaf-skirts, the conch-shell bangles, her teeth like rice sprouts, her skin like young mango leaf, her great shoulders and red-streaked eyes, and in one poem even the taste of her saliva—yet a woman is never described in more than one or two details in each poem. We do not hear much about the man's appearance; we know more about what he has and about his country's scenery than about him. As we hear about her glittering bangles and ornaments, we also hear of his bright spear, his horses, chariots, garlands, anklebands, sometimes a chest enlarged by the drawing of bows. His spouse's chastiny and virtue are also a chieftain's ornaments and his magical shields against disaster, as effective as his own "upright scepter" (*cenkol,* as contrasted with *kotunkol* "crooked scepter"). It is significant that in the *akam* poems, rarely is the woman seen as the mature mother

> of a grown man, as she is in the *puram*. As in other heroic milieus, women bards, and poems in women's voices, enlist filiat and familial feeling in the cause of war-especially that most compelling of family feeling, a mother's pride (or shame) about her son. (Devy 373-74)

Ramanujan is his essay, "The Ring of Memory" (Remembering and forgetting in Indian Literatures) analysis how memory and the loss of it are the roots of ancient Indian literature and particularly, Kalidasa's *Sakuntala*. Memory is an art that forms part of 'ancient classical and oral traditions'. Ramanujan observes:

> We know that the Vedas were orally transmitted for centuries before they were written down; even after they were written down they were systematically memorized, gotten by heart, inscribed as it were on the bodies of the reciters. The techniques for acquiring them orally included not only grammatical and phonetic analyses, but various pedagogic methods of marking each uttered phrase physically by various gestures and bodily movements—so that the texts were inscribed almost into the body's motor memory. (Daniels-Ramanujan and Keith Harrison 84)

Not remembering the past, opens the floodgate of repeating the past and pastmistakes. Ramanujan mentions Santayana and Freud to reinforce his observations. Our past, present and future are examined in terms of memory associations with reference to birth, death and rebirth. Ramanujan explains:

> In Hindu, Jaina or Buddhist conceptions of karma, unacknowledged past actions have a way of imposing their structure on the present, usually with the subject and object reversed, with oneself as the victim and one's former victim as the aggressor in life after life. Thus one's deeds or karma as well as one's memories have a pattern in common: deeds leave behind traces called *samskaras,* which persist in future lives, and *uasanas,* or smells of the past. It is through these that the past structure is revived, whether in memory or in the working of karma. Only awareness, recollection, remembering, rising beyond one's 'natural' tendency to forget and erase, only such

> an act of knowing can release one from the thralldom of repetition and rebirth. (Daniels-Ramanujan and Keith Harrison 86)

In Indian love poetry the absent presence (Derrida would be happy about it) plays a vital role. We know many of our great love poems are poems of separation. Ramanujan speaks of texts generating other texts which are new creations in Indian context. That is why we call translation as 'new writing', 'creative writing' in India not imitations. In "Three Hundred Ramayanas: Five Examples and Three Thoughts on Translation". Ramanujan tells us of different *Ramayanas* in our country. He writes:

> One day when Rama was sitting on his throne, his ring fell off. When it touched the earth, it made a hole in the ground and disappeared into it. It was gone. His trusty henchman, Hanuman, was at his feet. Rama said to Hanuman, 'Look, my ring is lost, find it for me'. (Dharwadker 131)

When Hanuman went in search of the ring, he met the king of spirits, who asked him to recognize the ring.

> The king looked around and showed him a platter. On it were thousands of rings. They were all Rama's rings. The king brought the platter to Hanuman, Shaking his head.
>
> The King of Spirit said, 'There have been an many Ramas as there are rings on this platter. When you return to earth, you will not find Rama. This incarnation of Rama is now over. Whenever an incarnation of Rama is about to be over, his ring falls down. I collect them and keep them. Now you can go'. (Dharwadker 133)

Ramanujan understands Indian literature by going to the roots and explains it with clarity and precision.

To conclude, I should say that Sri Aurobindo and Ramanujan have originality and critical insight that enable us to interpret Indian literature more fruitfuly than the theories of the Western Critics. Nissim Ezekiel's Criticism is based partly on his own experience as a poet and partly on the Western Criticism.

WORKS CITED

Becker, A.L. and Keith Taylor. "Interview Two". *Uncollected Poems and Prose*. Ed. Molly Daniels-Ramanujan and Keith Harrison. Delhi: OUP, 2001 rpt, 2005. Print.

Dharwadker, Vinay, ed. *The Collected Essays of A.K. Ramanujan*, Delhi: OUP, 1999. Print.

Ezekiel, Nissim. *Selected Prose*. Delhi: OUP, 1992. Print.

Ramanujan, A.K. "On Ancient Tamil Poetics". *Indian Literary Criticism*. Ed. G.N. Devy. Hyderabad: Orient Longman Pvt. Ltd., 2002. Print.

——. "The Ring of Memory". *Uncollected Poems and Prose*. Ed. Molly Daniels-Ramanujan and Keith Harrison, Delhi: OUP, 2005. Print.

Sri Aurobindo. *The Future Poetry*, Vol. 9, 1972. Print.

——. "The Sources of Poetry", *Indian Literary Criticism*. Ed. G.N. Devy. Hyderabad: Orient Longman Pvt. Ltd., 2002. Print.

10

The Centripetal/The Centrifugal Force in C.D. Narasimhaiah's Criticism

Criticism without scholarship is hollow and scholarship without critical insight is shallow. It is said that Oxford gives one knowledge but Cambridge gives one the sense of critical discrimination. C.D.N. (as C.D. Narasimhaiah is affectionately called) possessed both knowledge from wide reading and the critical acumen from his Cambridge training. It is also said in another context that one cannot teach effectively without doing research and one cannot do meaningful research without teaching. C.D.N. combined both teaching and research in his long and admirable academic life. In him, scholarship and criticism, teaching and research are all wedded together. No wonder, he published such scholarly books as *The Swan and the Eagle* (1968), *The Function of Criticism in India* (1986), *Essays in Commonwealth Literature* (1995), *Raja Rao* (1973), *Jawaharlal Nehru* (2001), *Moving Frontiers of English Studies in India* (1977), *Indian Critical Scene: Controversial Essays* (1990) and edited equally scholarly books titled, *Awakened Conscience* (1978): *East West Poetics at Work* (1994), and *Makers of Indian English Literature* (2001) and an admirable anthology called, *An Anthology of Commonwealth Poetry* (1990), besides scores of scholarly papers and illuminating editorials in his own influential *The Literary Criterion* which he founded in 1952. One can't help saying, 'here is God's plenty'.

Narasimhaiah is well versed in Western criticism. There is no west bashing in his criticism. Like Jawaharlal Nehru, whom he liked immensely, he believed in acquiring knowledge from the west but he lamented the loss of our inheritance—the critical sense locked in Sanskrit poetics. F.R. Leavis is a formidable influence on Narasimhaiah. It is from him that Narasimhaiah learnt the challenging act of discrimination and value judgement. He was influenced by Matthew Arnold and T.S. Eliot too. But it is his knowledge of Indian Poetics and Sri Aurobindo's criticism that made him discover his roots. He draws a parallel between American New Criticism (Formalism) and Indian Poetics in the following words:

> The so-called New Critics of America, very new indeed and some very green, perpetrated critical monism, each affirming the primacy of his own approach: Irony, Paradox, Texture, Tension, Ambiguity—reducing literary criticism to a mental exercise, while from Bharata, Dandin, Bhamaha, Vamana to Kuntaka, Anandavardhana, Abhinavagupta, Kshemendra, Rajashekhara and Viswanatha, whether one talked of Rasa, Riti, Guna, Alankara, Aucitya, Dhvani, they never missed the end in view, namely *rasanubhava,* the imaginative experience of a work of art. As if to tie up the beginning and the end Abhinavagupta coined the compound term Rasa-Dhvani, reflecting completeness of response, incomparably more complex than what was known to that "master of the sapient throng", the father of all that know, with his simplistic but enormously, embarrassingly, influential theory of catharsis as the product of pity and fear. (*The Function of Criticism in India* 15-16)

Narasimhaiah has high praise for Sri Aurobindo whom he compares with Eliot and Leavis as a critic and whose *Future Poetry* demonstrates, "a rare mastery of the whole range of British Poetry" (88). Sri Aurobindo has made certain observations on the poet, his personality and the tradition to which he belongs which run parallel to Eliot's idea of tradition and the individual talent and impersonal theory of poetry. He states that the poet depends not only on himself and the age but 'the mentality of the nation to which he belongs' and he has a dual personality that of the normal man and the 'seer of things'. How close he is to Eliot!

Narasimhaiah knows that Western criticism is in vogue in our time and country. He also knows that the schools of criticism are time bound. He clearly states it in *The Function of Criticism in India*:

> Concepts and approaches of a succession of critical positions such as Naturalism, Contextualism, Marxism, Phenomenology, Eschotology, Structuralism, Deconstruction have all had their passing appeal by turns even as the West was getting rid of them. (22)

What irks more is our dependence on the West for their critical evaluation of our literature. We have not yet got rid of the colonial mentality—that is, the west knows best not only about themselves but about us as well. Narasimhaiah underlines this point in the following paragraph from *The Function of Criticism in India*:

> The *Vedas* were great because Max Muller said so, the *Upanishads* endured because Schopenhauer and Deussen and Yeats thought well of them. The *Gita* and the Buddha came to the English educated Indian, including Gandhi and Nehru—it couldn't have been different to most of us, Western-educated Indians-thanks to Edwin Arnold's *Song Celestial* and *Light of Asia*. Tagore was great because W.B. Yeats thought so. The *Brihadaranyaka Upanishad* acquired a sudden importance because of T.S. Eliot's *Datta, Dayadhvam, Damyata*. The *Gita* gained the distinction of poetry, because the most important poet of the age thought it was 'the second greatest philosophical poem of the world'. (211)

Now let us take Narasimhaiah's criticism of Indian English literature beginning with his seminal book, *The Swan and the Eagle*. Here, having defined Indian English literature, he evaluates the poetry of Sarojini Naidu, Toru Dutt, Sri Aurobindo, Dom Moraes, Nissim Ezekiel, P. Lal, the prose of Swami Vivekananda, Jawaharlal Nehru, Nirad C. Chaudhuri, the novels of Mulk Raj Anand, R.K. Narayan, Raja Rao, Salman Rushdie, Vikram Seth, Shashi Tharoor, and Arundhati Roy with insight and precision. M.K. Naik calls it 'rather sketchy' (*The Journal of Indian Writing in English*. Jan. 2006; 2). Not to speak of other chapters, if

Naik had cared to read Narasimhaiah's analysis of Sarojini Naidu's "Weavers', Toru Dutt's 'Lotus', Sri Aurobindo's *Savitri*, Raja Rao's *The Serpent and the Rope*, thoroughly he would have realized the importance of Narasimhaiah as a critic. I sometimes wonder how Sahitya Akademi could have ignored Narasimhaiah, when it honoured two other critics, G.N. Devy for *After Ammesia* in 1993 and Meenakshi Mukherjee for *The Perishable Empire* in 2003 respectively. Narasimhaiah likes Nehru, Anand, Narayan and particularly Raja Rao and comes down heavily on Nirad C. Chaudhuri, Salman Rushdie, Vikram Seth, Shashi Tharoor and Arundhati Roy (the last four in chapter X of the book under the title, "Spurious Reputations"). Of Nehru he writes approvingly:

> Nature has held the greatest fascination for poets in India from Valmiki and Kalidasa to their descendants today, but not without deteriorating quite often into ornamental descriptions without function in the context. Nehru can get away with successive paragraphs at a stretch and make them all convincing to the reader when he excuses himself: 'prevented from indulging in normal activities we became more observant of nature's ways'. Not just plausible but very convincing in the circumstances. For, prison life which can deaden most sensitive natures seems to have afforded an exceptional opportunity for Nehru to watch landscape, insects, birds and beasts and how they minister to his need or mould his character. (*The Swan and the Eagle* 135)

In *The God of Small Things,* Narasimhaiah finds the description of place, 'May in Ayemenem is a hot brooding month' in chapter I wrong. He concludes:

> There was a good chance that The God of Great Things, He with His Four Hands, would have helped Roy to save Ammu from flirting with the 'god of one arm' (217) and herself look up for stimulus, to Toru Dutt, that child prodigy, also a convert to Christianity, to impart a touch of Nachiketa and Savitri to her twins, Rahel and Estha, now left fretting against their mother for being 'diddled out of free bus-rides for life' and cheated Roy herself

> into being the recipient of Booker Prize, worth no more than baker's burnt bread, before the ceiestial gift. (*The Swan and the Eagle* 257)

Narasimhaiah analyses Nehru's writings dispassionately and admires the latter's attempt at synthesizing the ideas of the East and West in his *An Autobiography, Glimpses of World History* and *The Discovery of India.* Nehru had incorporated quotations from GM. Hopkins's Sonnets, and T.S. Eliot's *Hollow Men* and *Four Quartets.* What impressed more, says Narasimhaiah is, a Western-educated man with a scientific temper, Nehru, 'worked hard to absorb the valid tradition of India from the *Upanishads* to Aurobindo, Radhakrishnan and Coomaraswamy' (Jawaharlal Nehru 12). What is admirable in Nehru is his effort to 'make the past meaningful to the present' and hence we find in *The Discovery of India,* 'accounts of the *Vedas,* the *Upanishads* and the *Epics,* the early civilization of the Indus valley, the teachings of the Buddha and Mahavira, the successive invasions of India by outsiders and India's contact with other nations' (Jawaharlal Nehru 122). What is rewarding in the book is not only Narasimhaiah's analysis of Nehru's literary writings but his letters and speeches which are equally valuable as literature. Narasimhaiah found that English literature has reached its dead end with the Victorians-Arnold, Hardy and the moderns—Eliot, Joyce and the like, and it was losing its appeal to the Indians, so he turned to American literature with his training at Princeton University and popularized it in India. But wherein lies his forte, is not American literature but Commonwealth Literature. It is he, who brought Commonwealth literature to Indian classrooms and worked on it in his scholarly *The Literary Criterion.* The result is his book, titled *Essays in Commonwealth Literature* (1995) and his admirably edited volume, *The Awakened Conscience* which he edited as the Chairman of IACLALS (Narasimhaiah organized IACLALS Triennial Conference in New Delhi in 1977). He discussed African Literature, Australian Literature, Literatures of Asia-Pacific Region, Canadian Poetry, New Zealand Poetry and Indian English literature and evaluated A.D. Hope, Derek Walcott, V.S. Naipaul, Chinua Achebe, Wole Soyinka, R.K. Narayan and a few others in *Essays in Commonwealth Literature.* In a very perceptive chapter of this book, "Commonwealth Literature: Heirloom of Multiple Heritage", he observes:

> The Commonwealth offers possibilities for intelligent meeting of the East and the West through a yet unexplored territory which has held out promise of fruitful interaction in the ancient world by possible contact between Hellenic and Hindu ideas. The parallels are striking. Plato's concepts of 'Idea' and 'Imitation', after all, have their parallels—Bernth Lindfors remarks, the lines can be oblique, not always parallel—in the mainstream of the Indian thought from the Upanishads and Sankara to the present day. Both Aristotle's *Poetics* and Bharatha's *Natyasastra,* treatises on dramaturgy, use biological and mental images. While Aristotle made plot the soul of Tragedy, Bharatha offers *rasa,* (literally juice) a state beyond pain and pleasure. And while Aristotle apparently simplifies tragic experience by restricting it to the two dominant emotions of pity and fear, Bharatha enumerates eight primary emotions (to which a ninth has been added by subsequent authorities) and any number of fleeting emotions, validated by modern European psychologists like McDougall. More, Bharatha has given the world such an invaluable critical tool as *Vibhava,* the 'objective correlative' to which T.S. Eliot has given wide currency in our own times and the resultant generation of the *rasa,* the aesthetic state of the reader, made memorable by Matthew Arnold in the celebrated phrase 'Indian virtue of detachment'. (*Essays in Commonwealth Literature* 43-44)

Mention may be made here of his admirable *An Anthology of Commonwealth Poetry* (1990), which he edited with introduction to individual sections besides a general introduction. No wonder, he brought poets from Africa, Australia, Canada, India, New Zealand, Pakistan, Bangladesh, Singapore, Malaysia, Sri Lanka and West Indies under one umbrella. Needless to say that it found its way to the syllabuses of Indian Universities as a textbook. Along with K.R.S. Iyengar, C.D. Narasimhaiah gave as it were 'a local habitation and a name' to Indian English Literature. In his numerous articles and books like *The Swan and the Eagle* and *Raja Rao* and through several lectures all over the country, Narasimhaiah has espoused the cause of Indian English Literature. Then came his well edited book of criticism. *Makers of Indian English Literature* (2000). Narasimhaiah seeks to find who are the real makers of Indian English literature. He comes down heavily on Indian English poets for their failure to attract the reading public. He writes:

> Too much preciosity and preoccupation with word play and too little experience to share with readers. This is so from Dom Moraes downwards to Nissim Ezekiel (with the solitary exception of *The Night of the Scorpion*) Keki Daruwalla, Jayanta Mahapatra and Shiv K. Kumar. While R. Parthasarathy is aware of their 'whoring after foreign gods' he too succumbs in practice to what he finds fault with. Only one poet, Kamala Das, comes through unscathed. Consequently Indian English Poetry hasn't gone beyond the bounds of prescriptive reading in classrooms where it figures because it must for want of better poetry. It has just not come out of the Academia to catch the interest of the intelligent general reader. It can be said without exaggeration that hardly a single poem of these poets figures on the Indian horizon for us to point to and take comfort in. And if their names are heard here and there they owe it to the Sahitya Akademi or the Commonwealth Foundation which award prizes annually, because they must observe the ritual! It may amuse us but it is true that Australian poets have given more memorable poems by using Indian material than all the Indian poets of the same period put together. One has in mind A.D. Hope's *Salabanjaka* and *Moschus Moscheferus,* Rodney Hall's *The Law of Karma,* and Les Murray's *Cow Poems.* (*Makers of Indian English Literature* 34)

Having mentioned some of Narasimhaiah's observations from his criticism, let me say a few words about his method of criticism. His approach is always comparative. He evaluates one writer with reference to another to show their merits as well as limitations. In his speech and also in his writing there is always a wide range of allusions, anecdotes to illustrate his point. His texts are replete with intersexuality. Scholarship and Criticism go together with him. He makes use of his learning in his writing. English for him is the 'other' through which he discovered his own roots. English made him critical of the West and also critical of ourselves. English is the centripetal force in his writing that tends to move away from the centre (i.e., India) and our own Indian Literary tradition; Sanskrit poetics and Sri Aurobindo's Criticism are the centrifugal force that brings him back to the centre. Like Nehru, Narasimhaiah wants to bring the things that we don't have from the West but retain the best that we have with us. In a way, he is with Gunter Grass who said, 'For God's sake, open the universe a little more'.

WORKS CITED

Narasimhaiah, C.D. *Raja Rao.* Indian Writers Series. New Delhi: Arnold Heinemann, 1973. Print.

——. *The Function of Criticism in India: Essays in Indian Response to Literature.* Mysore, CIIL, 1986. Print.

——. *Essays in Commonwealth Literature: Heirloom of Multiple Heritage.* Delhi: Pencraft International, 1995. Print.

——. *The Swan and the Eagle: Essays on Indian English Literature.* 3rd edn. Delhi: Vision Books, 1999. Print.

——. ed. *The Awakened Conscience.* New Delhi: Sterling Publishers, 1978. Print.

——. ed. *An Anthology of Commonwealth Poetry.* Madras: Macmillan India Ltd., 1990. Print.

11

Glocalization and the Eclipse of Postcolonial Theory

Globalization is an economic term which means that the prosperous West has entered into the East for the purpose of trade and business. Localization lays stress on indigenous qualities but the local now makes way to the West. The portmanteau word 'glocalization' comes out of two words 'globalization' and 'localization' meaning the import and export of trade, culture and literature from the west to the east and vice versa. The purpose of this chapter is to examine the beginning, growth and development of postcolonial literatures and the resultant postcolonial theory across the world.

The word 'postcolonial' is three dimensional. Historically, it means the end of colonial era, and becomes synonymous with post-independence for the erstwhile colonies. Theoretically, it makes use of some of the traits of post-structuralism and goes along with it. In the realms of literature, it used to be a synonym for Commonwealth Literature but the nomenclature of this literature and the identity of the writers belonging to erstwhile British and French colonies opened up new possibilities. English language writers across the world, because of migration in the second-half of the twentieth century defy exact classification. What does post-colonial theory mean? More importantly, when does post-colonialism begin? Britain was a colony of Rome and US too was a colony. But we never talk of post-colonial era in Britain and US. The word post-colonial first finds a mention in a British newspaper in 1959.

Dennis Walder and Nayantara Sahgal candidly express their views on the rise of the term post-colonial in the following passages:

> The OED records the first use of 'post-colonial' in a British newspaper article of 1959, referring to India, the jewel in the crown of Empire, which achieved independence in 1947; since when 'post-colonial' has referred mainly to the former colonized areas of Asia and Africa as they became self-governing states during the 1950s and 1960s—states as different yet related by their pasts as, say, Ghana and Singapore, or Pakistan and Sierra Leone. More recently, 'post-colonial' has come to be thought appropriate, because of the implication that the colonial experience persists despite the withdrawal of political control, as a result of the continuing strategic and economic power of the former colonizers, the new global dispositions which keep groups of poorer states in thrall; and because, as Sahgal admits, however minimal the impact of empire upon a particular people in the long perspective, it has always left its imprint (Walder 3).

Addressing the Silver Jubilee Conference of ACLALS (Association for Commonwealth Literature and Language Studies) at the University of Kent, Canterbury in August 1989, Nayantara Sahgal puts things in historical perspective under the caption, "The Schizophrenic Imagination" published in *From Commonwealth to Post-Colonial* edited by Anna Rutherford in 1992. She says.

> First we were colonials, and now we seem to be post-colonials. So in 'post-colonial' the new Anno Domini from which events are to be everlastingly measured? My own awareness as a writer reaches back to x-thousand BC, at the very end of which measureless timeless time the British came, and stayed, and left. And now they're gone, and their residue is simply one more layer added to the layer upon layer of Indian consciousness. Just one more. (qtd. in Walder 1)

From the above two observations, it is evident that 'post-colonial' is not post-independence because it is not the end of the 'colonialism'. The ideas of the colonial world continues to haunt the postcolonial pushing it to the world of neo-colonialism. People ask, "Is not post-colonial, still colonial?"

Newzealand, Australia, Canada were settler colonies, whereas Indian was a colony of conquest like other Asian and African countries. For the people of conquest colonies, post-colonialism begins after the Second World War. According to Homi K. Bhabha, "the term postcolonial is increasingly used to describe that form of social criticism that bears witness to those unequal and uneven processes of representation by which the historical experience of the once-colonized Third World comes to be framed in the West" (Mariani 63). To a question, 'When is post-coloniality supposed to have begun?' Arif Dirlik replied "When the Third World intellectuals have arrived in First World Academe". But when Lorna Goodson asked "When is postcoloniality going to end? How long does the post-colonial continue?" (Mongia 2) there seems to be no answer. Elleke Boehmer makes a valid observation in the following words:

> the term post-colonial still draws support for its usefulness as an umbrella term, a way of bracketing together the literatures written in those countries which were once colonies of Britain. The United States is excluded because it won independence long before other colonial places, and its literature has therefore followed a very different trajectory. Ireland too is believed to represent a different case because its history has been so closely and so long linked to that of Britain (4).

As postcolonialism has now resulted in neo-colonialism, the relevance of post-colonial theory to contemporary literary studies stands eclipsed under shadow of globalization and more importantly glocalization. Leading English language writers from Australia, Africa, West Indies, India, Pakistan and Sri Lanka are now living either in UK or in USA or dividing their time between UK and USA on the one hand and their homeland on the other. So immigrant, expatriate and diasporic writers in English in the twenty-first century defy an exact definition of their own identity as writers and the nomenclature of their writings becomes problematic. The theory of orientalism, hybridity, subaltern, catachresis are now in the wane. The wheel has turned a full circle. It is not the colonizers who are 'going nalive' but the writers of once colonized countries who are trying to appropriate themselves to the Western literary world. Even our IT engineers, doctors and intellectuals who work in the west, never return home. The question of centre/periphery, self and other has lost its relevance in the present context.

Let me refer to two significant points made by Salman Rushdie in his well-known book, *Imaginary Homelands*. He says,

> In my own case, I have constantly been asked whether I am British, or Indian. The formulation 'Indian-born British writer' has been invented to explain me. But, as I said last night, my new book deals with Pakistan. So what now? 'British-resident Indo-Pakistani writer'? You see the folly of trying to contain writers inside passports. (67)
>
> As for myself, I don't think it is always necessary to take up the anti-colonial—or is it post-colonial?—cudgels against English. What seems to me to be happening is that those peoples who were once colonized by the language are now rapidly remaking it, domesticating it, becoming more and more relaxed about the way they use it—assisted by the English language's enormous flexibility and size, they are carving out large territories for themselves within its frontiers. (64)

The statements of Rushdie (who is regarded as the leader of new Indian diaspora) bear testimony to the points I have made in this chapter.

Globalization is another form of neo-colonialism. The concept of 'home' has undergone a sea change. Now the arguments made regarding home seem to be dated. They are, 'home is where the heart is', 'home is where the mind is', 'home is where the feet are' and finally, 'home is where the women are'. Because, a man builds a house but it is the woman who makes a home of it. Here comes to our mind, Bhabha's 'Third Space' and the mythical Indian character Trishankhu', who was suspended between two worlds—the earth and heaven. Critics think that all diasporic writers long to return home, which is not the case. R. Parthasarathy does not intend to return to India nor did Raja Rao. Bharati Mukherjee says that, 'well-bred post-colonials much like myself, adrift in the new world' (qtd. in Walder 1). Salman Rushdie being very practical says that it is not possible to return to the past because it is for him, 'a lost home in a lost city in the mist of lost time' (9). He elaborates this idea in the following passage:

> It may be that writers in my position, exiles or emigrants or expatriates, are haunted by some sense of loss, some urge to reclaim, to look back, even at the risk of being mutated into pillars of salt. But if we do look back, we must also do so in the knowledge—which gives rise to profound uncertainties—that our physical alienation from India almost inevitably means that we will not be capable of reclaiming precisely the thing that was lost; that we will, in short, create fictions, not actual cities or villages, but invisible ones, imaginary homelands, Indias of the mind. (10)

If for Salman Rushdie being out of the country as an exile, emigrant or expatriate is a sense of loss, for Ramanujan it is an advantage. In course of an interview to A.L. Becker and Keith Taylor, Ramanujan says,

> I don't even call myself an expatriate, because I've done a lot of work on India since coming to this country. I've done it more comfortably here than I could even have done it in India. For instance, in the Chicago Regenstein Library, there are books in Kannada and Tamil which probably only I will read. It's a great library that is more or less only for a couple of people like me. When I went to Delhi—I was working on some classical Tamil poems—I had to go for miles to find a classical Tamil book.
>
> And the other interesting thing is that one can be an internal alien in India, as one goes from one province to another. I have not lived in my own language region

> since my 20th year. If you go a hundred miles away, you are in a language that you cannot read or speak. (Daniels-Ramanujan and Harrison 52-53)

Edward Said's terms such as 'Orientalism', 'Contrapuntal reading' and 'imperialism' help us to understand our position vis-a-vis the West. Orientalism is based on the Western view of the East as inferior to the West. But this is not true. When we go back in time through history we find our vibrant culture and literature. So we begin to write alternative history. Our great literature enables us to see into the past and makes us proud of our ancestors. Each country in Asia, and Africa, West Indies leaving aside the settler colonies wants to identify its own literature in indigenous terms. If Commonwealth Literature does not exit, postcolonial literature now ceases to exist. A.K. Ramanujan makes a valid point when he takes English as the 'other' through which we have discovered ourselves. He writes:

> English has been the 'other' through which we have returned to ourselves. English has become a part of us. To say we want to return to a pre-English state is chimerical. The anti-colonial discourse is all done in English. Nobody's writing this in Kannada. In India, there is a wonderful group of new historians called the Subalterns, who are looking at all the distortions of the colonial intellectual practices.
>
> But all their work is done in English. Isn't the English in which they are writing distorting what they are writing about? English has made us self-critical and made us critical of English itself. (Daniels-Ramanujan and Harrison 79)

Erstwhile British colonies have adopted English as their own language, mostly the second language in which the new generations of people in their respective countries have received their education. That being the situation, their writers have chosen to write in that language. Take the case of Indian English writers. The language is English (not Queen's English) but the expression is Indian. They have moulded the English language in such a way that it became a vehicle to carry native expression without mimicry of English writers.

In India apart from Indian English writers, the Bhasha writers are also getting their works translated into English. The paradox is that the Bhasha writers who were sceptical of Indian English writers for their lack of authenticity, now get their works translated into English for the purpose of international visibility. English language has been made flexible by writers from developing countries. English has become ours, it is now no less important for us than it used to be.

Using native idioms the writers of erstwhile British colonies give feedback to the English speaking world on "the myths, legends and superstitions of older and mature societies as is evident in the works of Achebe, Soyinka, and Clark from Africa, Anand, Narayan, Raja Rao, Desani and Kamala Markandaya of India, Lamming, Naipaul, Harris and Brathwaite of West Indies" (Narasimhaiah 7).

In *Salman Rushdie and the Third World* (1989) Timothy Bernnan proposed a new title for the writers of the erstwhile colonies, Meenakshi Mukherjee has rightly pointed out this in her book titled, *The Perishable Empire: Essays Indian Writing in English* in the following words:

> In 1989 Timothy Brennan proposed a new category of novelists: the 'Third World Cosmopolitans', who are globally visible, whom the reviewers in *New York* and *London Review of Books* hail as interpreters and authentic voices of the 'Third World'. According to Bernnan, this group includes Mario Vargas Llosa, Derek Walcott, Salman Rushdie, Isabel Allende, Gabriel Garcia Marquez and Bharati Mukherjee, but not Chinua Achebe or Wole Soyinka. If he wrote his book a few years later he might have added the names of Ben Okri. Robert Antoni, Michael Ondaatje and a few others. The Third World cosmopolitans emerge from a non-western culture, but their mastery over the current idiom of the metropolitan meta-language of narrative ensures their favourable reception in the global centres

> of publication and criticism. It should also be noted that not all outstanding writers from other cultures (writing in English or translated into English) receive this attention. The new receptivity in London or New York may have made it easier for some writers from outside the western world to get a hearing, but they may do so only within a field of reception already defined by metropolitan parameters and agendas. The criteria of evaluation are naturally selective, determined by the demands of the recipient culture. (178-79)

Now we have two categories of writings—one, originally in English and another equally vibrant literature rendered into English available for readers in English across the world. Then the question arises: can we apply postcolonial theory to neo-colonial and global writings in English and do justice to the new writers (as well as established writers)? The nomenclature of literature cannot be described in terms of visa or passport. Both the country of a writer's origin and the country of his/her current habitation should go together to decide the nomenclature of his/her writing. V.S. Naipaul's dedication of his Nobel Prize to both the country of his living (England) and 'the country of his origin' (India) seems to be a way out.

Postcolonial theory of dividing the people of the world in terms of domination and subservience, white and black, knowledge and ignorance no longer holds good. Glocalization has become an anti-dote to globalization. The former colonies are now asserting themselves by going into their own roots and rediscovering their indigenous history, culture and literature. There are three important reasons for which post-colonialism is now getting eclipsed. One, each country of the former colonies is trying to evaluate its literature according to is own critical canon—not according to Anglo-American critical tradition. That is why, there is so much emphasis on culture—indigenous as well as multiculturalism. The emphasis is now to evaluate literature through culture. The factors which normally go into the making of literature are now highlighted more than literature proper. For example, Africans feel bold enough to evaluate their literature in accordance with their own indigenous culture and tradition.

What Chinua Achebe said in an interview to Kwame Anthony Appiah in 1982, seems to be valid for all categories of English language writers (exiles, emigrants, expatriates and diasporans):

> I am an Ibo writer because this is my basic culture; Nigerian, African and a writer...no, black first, then a writer. Each of these identities does call for a certain kind of commitment on my part. I must see what it is to be black—and this means sufficiently intelligent to know how the world is moving and how the black people fare in this world. This is what it means to be black. Or an African—what does Africa mean to the world? When you see an African, what does it mean to a white man. (qtd. in Innes 208)

Two, the writers belonging to erstwhile colonies employ English language in their own way. Thus, we find Indian English, African English, Caribbean English as the medium of creative writing in their respective countries. Three, globalization and internet have brought information for all, both in the east and in the west. Knowledge is no longer the monopoly of the elite west. Moreover many Third World Writers are now living in the west. Postcolonial literature is now overshadowed by the translation of canonical texts of indigenous literature into English. Moreover, now post-colonial literature is now treated not as one homogenous unity but a heterogenous body of writings done in English in erstwhile British and French Colonies. Each country wants its literature to be named after the country and continents —African literature, Indian English literature, Caribbean literature, Australian literature, Canadian literature so on and so forth. Therefore, postcolonial criticism, which is socio-political criticism cannot be applied to literature of different countries. Eco-criticism, new historicism and globalization theories have gone beyond post-colonial theory. In postcolonial criticism what had already been said long ago is still being said. So this kind of criticism loses its significance in the age of globalization—more importantly glocalization. It is the migrant writers—exiles, expatriates, immigrants, and diasporic—who are now globally visible. Elsewhere I have stated it clearly in the following passage:

> Expatriate writer is one who voluntarily leaves the country to promote his/her career and keeps the option open to return home. A.K. Ramanujan, R. Parthasarathy, Meena Alexander, Raja Rao, Kiran Desai belong to this category. Bapsi Sidhwa, Bharati Mukherjee, Rohinton Mistry, Salman Rushdie, V.S. Naipaul, Ben Okri, Ngugi wa Thiong'o, Michael Ondaatje belong to the category of emigrant or immigrant writers. V.S. Naipaul for us is a diasporic writer, and for the Caribbeans an emigrant writer. The diasporic writers are those whose ancestors have left for another country. Salman Rushdie can also be treated as writer in exile for almost a decade. The boundaries of literatures in English by these English language writers of all varieties (expatriate, exile, emigrant, immigrant and diasporic) are blurring. Moreover, there are some writers who divide their time between UK, USA and their homeland. To this category belong many African, Caribbean and Indian writers. Names of Anita Desai, Vikram Seth, Vikram Chandra, Amitav Ghosh, George Lamming, Chinua Achebe and Derek Walcott can be cited in this context. (Das 173-74)

Previously the identity of literature used to be determined according to nationality, culture and language. Now in the age of glocalization this identity should be determined on the basis of origin, current habitation and language of the writer. Hence, postcolonial theory will have limited validity in the changing scenario.

WORKS CITED

Bhabha, Homi K. '"Caliban Speaks to Prospero": Cultural Identity and the Crisis of Representations'. *Critical Fictions*. Ed. Phil Mariani. Seattle: Bey Press, 1991. Print.

Das, Bijay Kumar. *Critical Essays on Post-Colonial Literature*. New Delhi: Atlantic Publishers, 2012. Print.

Elleke, Boehmer. *Colonial and Postcolonial Literature*. Oxford: OUP, 1995. Print.

Innes, C.L. *The Cambridge Introduction to Post-Colonial Literatures in English*. New Delhi: Cambridge University Press, 2008. Print.

Mongia, Padmini. ed. *Contemporary Postcolonial Theory: A Reader.* Delhi: Oxford University Press, 1997. Print.

Mukherjee, Meenakshi. *The Perishable Empire.* Delhi: OUP, 2000. Print.

Narasimhaiah, C.D., ed. *Commonwealth Literature: A Handbook of Select Reading Lists.* Delhi: OUP, 1976. Print.

Ramanujan, A.K. "Interview Two". *Uncollected Poems and Prose.* Eds. Molly Daniels-Ramanujan and Keith Harrison. New Delhi: OUP, 2001. Print.

Rushdie, Salman. *Imaginary Homelands: Essays and Criticism 1981-1991.* London: Granta Books, 1991 rpt. 1992. Print.

Walder, Dennis. *Post-Colonial Literatures in English:* New Delhi: Atlantic Publishers, 2002 rpt. 2005. Print.

Select Bibliography

Andrews, Elmer, ed. *Seamus Heaney: A Collection of Critical Essays*. Basingstoke and London: Macmillan, 1992.

Ashcroft, Bill, Gareth Griffiths, and Helen Tiffin. *The Empire Writes Back: Theory and Practice in Post-Colonial Literatures*. London and New York: Routledge, 1989.

——. eds. *The Post-colonial Studies Reader*. London and New York: Routledge, 1995.

——. *Postcolonial Studies: The Key Concepts*. London and New York: Routledge, 1998.

Bertens, Hans. *Literary Theory: The Basics*. London: Routledge, 2001.

Bloom, Harold et al. *Deconstruction and Criticism*. London: Routledge and Kegan Paul, 1979.

——. ed. *T.S. Eliot*. Broomall: Chelsea House Publishers, 2003.

——. *The Anxiety of Influence: A Theory of Poetry*. New York: Oxford University Press, 1973.

——. *A Map of Misreading*. New York: Oxford University Press, 1975.

——. *The Western Canon: The Books and School of Ages*. London: MacMillan, 1995.

Boehmer, Elleke. *Colonial and Postcolonial Literature*. Oxford: Oxford University Press, 1995.

Booth, W.C. *Powers and Limits of Critical Pluralism*. Chicago: University of Chicago Press, 1979.

Burris, Sydney. *The Poetry of Resistance: Seamus Heaney and the Pastoral Tradition*. Athens, GA: Ohio University Press, 1990.

Das, Bijay Kumar. *Perspectives on Indian English Poetry Criticism*. Bareily: PBD, 1993.

——. *The Poetry of Jayanta Mahapatra*. (Third Revised Enlarged Edition), New Delhi: Atlantic Publishers, 2009.

——. Aspects of Commonwealth Literature. New Delhi: Creative Books, 1995.

——. *The Horizon of Nissim Ezekiel's Poetry*. New Delhi: B.R. Publishing Corporation, 1995.

——. *Shiv K. Kumar as a Postcolonial Poet*. New Delhi: Atlantic Publishers, 2001.

——. *Critical Essays on Poetry*. Ludhiana: Kalyani Publishers, 2003.

——. *Perspectives on the Poetry of A.K. Ramanujan:* New Delhi: Doaba House, 2013.

——. *Critical Essays on Postcolonial Literature*. New Delhi: Atlantic Publishers, 2009, rpt. 2012.

——. *Postmodern Indian English Literature*. New Delhi: Atlantic Publishers, 2006.

——. *Twentieth Century Literacy Criticism*. (7th Rev. and Enlarged Edn.), New Delhi: Atlantic Publishers, 2014.

——. ed. *New Readings in Indian English Literature*. Bareilly: Prakash Book Depot, 2011.

——. ed. *Perspectives on the Poetry of R. Parthasarathy*. Bareilly: PBD, 1977.

de Man, Paul. *The Resistance to Theory: Theory and History of Literature*. Manchester: Manchester University Press, 1986.

Durkan, Michael J. and Rand Brandes. *Seamus Heaney: A Reference Guide*. New York: G.K. Hall, 1995.

Eliot, T.S. *On Poetry and Poets*. London: Faber and Faber, 1957.

——. *Selected Essays*. New York: Harcourt, Brace, 1960.

Eliot, T.S. *The Use of the Poetry and the Use of Criticism.* London: Faber and Faber, 1933.

Faas, Ekbert. *Ted Hughes: The Unaccommodated Universe.* Santa Barbara, Calif: Black Sparrow Press, 1980.

Gandhi, Leela. *Postcolonial Theory: A Critical Introduction.* New Delhi: Oxford University Press, 1999.

Garratt, Robert F. ed. *Critical Essays on Seamus Heaney.* NY: G.K. Hall; London: Prentice-Hall, 1995.

Hart, Henry. *Seamus Heaney: Poet of Contrary Progressions.* Syracuse, NY: Syracuse University Press, 1992.

Iyengar, K.R.S. *Indian Writing in English.* Bombay: Asia Publishing House, 1962.

Jeffares, A. Norman. *The Circus Animals: Essays on W.B. Yeats.* London: MacMillan, 1970.

——. *Karnani, Chetan.* Nissim Ezekiel. Delhi: Arnold Heinemann, 1974.

Kenner, Hugh. *The Invisible Poet: T.S. Eliot.* London: W.H. Allen, 1960.

Kher, Indernath. ed. *Journal of South Asian Literature.* (Special Number on Ezekiel). Spring/Summer, 1976.

King, Bruce. *Modern Indian Poetry in English.* Delhi: Oxford University Press, 1987.

——. *Three Indian Poets.* Madras: OUP, 1991.

Kulshrestha, Chirantan, ed. *Contemporary Indian English Verse: An Evaluation*, 1980.

Lodge, David, ed. *20th Century Literary Criticism: A Reader.* London: Longman, 1989.

Loomba, Ania. *Colonialism/Postcolonialism.* New York: Routledge, 1999.

Lucy, Niall, ed. *Postmodern Literary Theory: An Introduction.* Oxford: Blackwell, 1997.

McDoland, Peter. *Serious Poetry: Form and Authority from Yeats to Hill.* Oxford: Oxford University Press, 2002.

Matthiessen, F.O. *The Achievement of T.S. Eliot.* London: Oxford University Press, 1958.

Mongia, Padmin, ed. *Contemporary Postcolonial Theory: A Reader.* New Delhi: Oxford University Press, 1997.

Naik, M.K. *A History of Indian English Literature.* New Delhi: Sahitya Akademi, 1982.

——. ed. *Aspects of Indian Writing in English.* New Delhi: Macmillan, 1979.

——. ed. *Perspectives on Indian Poetry in English.* New Delhi: Abhinav Publications, 1984.

Naik, M.K., S.K. Desai and G.S. Amur, ed. *Critical Essays on Indian Writing in English.* Dharwar: Karnatak University, 1968.

Naik, M.K. and Shyamala A. Narayan. *Indian English Literature: 1980-2000: A Critical Study.* New Delhi: Pencraft, 2001.

Newton, K.M., ed. *Contemporary Postcolonial Theory: A Reader.* London: Macmillan Press Ltd., 1997.

Nkrumah, K. *Neo-colonialism: The Last Stage of Imperialism.* London: Methuen, 1982.

O'Donoghue, Bernard, *Seamus Heaney and the Languages of Poetry.* Hemel Hempstead: Harvester Wheatsheaf, 1994.

Panikar, K. Ayyappa. ed. *Indian English Literature Since Independence.* New Delhi: IAES, 1990.

Parker, Michael, *Seamus Heaney: The Making of the Poet.* Dublin: Gill and Macmillan, 1993.

Parthasarathy, R. ed. *Ten Twentieth Century Indian Poets.* New Delhi: Oxford University Press, 1977.

Pinto, V. de S. *Crisis in English Poetry 1880-1940.* London: Hutchinson and Co. (Publishers) Ltd., 1967.

Roberts, Neil, ed. *A Companion to Twentieth-Century Poetry.* Melbourne: Blackwell Publishing Ltd., 2003.

Ricks, Christopher. *The Force of Poetry.* Oxford: Clarendon Press, 1984.

Sagar, Keith, ed. *The Challenge of Ted Huges.* Basingstoke: Macmillan, 1994.

Said, Edward. *Orientalism*. Harmondsworth: Penguin, 1978.

——. *The World, the Text and the Critic*. Cambridge, MA: Harvard University Press, 1983.

——. *Culture and Imperialism*. London: Chatto and Windus, 1993.

Spivak, Gayatri. *The Post-colonial Critic, Interviews, Strategies, Dialogues*. Ed. Sarah Harasym. New York: Routledge, 1990.

Smith, Grover Cuveland. *T.S. Eliot's Poetry and Plays: A Study in Sources and Meaning*. Chicago: The University of Chicago Press, 1956.

Tate, Allen, ed. *T.S. Eliot: The Man and His Work*. New York: Delacorte Press, 1966.

Unger, Leonard. *T.S. Eliot: Moment and Patterns*. Minneapolis: University of Minnerota Press, 1961.

Walder, Dennis. *Ted Hughes*. Milton Keynes: Open University Press, 1987.

Walsh, Williams. *Readings in Commonwealth Literature*. Oxford: Clarendon Press, 1973.

——. *Indian Literature in English*. London: Longman, 1990.

Wellek, Rene. *Concepts of Criticism*. New Haven: Yale University Press, 1963.

Yeats, W.B., ed. *The Oxford Book of Modern Verse*. Oxford: Clarendon Press, 1936.

Index